Prologue to the Future

The Japan Society is an association of Americans and Japanese actively engaged in bringing the peoples of their two nations closer together in understanding, appreciation and cooperation. Founded in 1907, it is a private, nonprofit, nonpolitical membership corporation organized under the laws of the State of New York, devoted to cultural, educational and public affairs, and to discussions, exchanges, and studies in areas of interest to both peoples. Its aim is to provide a medium through which each nation may learn from the experiences and accomplishments of the other. Japan House, the Society's new headquarters of contemporary Japanese design, located on Hammarskjold Plaza near the United Nations in New York City, was dedicated in September of 1971.

The Japan Society's Public Affairs Program, under which the materials for this publication were developed, aims to encourage informed public consideration of important issues involving Japan and the United States. This work is one in a series of Society Publications in the public affairs area. As with all Society publications, this work represents solely the findings and views of the authors concerned, and should not be construed to reflect the views of the Japan Society, Inc., its officers, directors, staff, or members.

Sponsored by Japan Society, Inc.

Mr. John D. Rockefeller 3rd   Mr. Isaac Shapiro
Chairman of the Board   President

Japan House, 333 East 47th Street, New York, N.Y. 10017

Prologue to the Future

The United States and Japan
in the Postindustrial Age

Edited by: James William Morley
Contributors: Charles Frankel
    Nathan Glazer
    Robert L. Heilbroner
    Samuel P. Huntington
    James William Morley
    Ken'ichi Tominaga
    Yoshimi Uchikawa
    Hirofumi Uzawa
    Joji Watanuki
Project Director: F. Roy Lockheimer

Published for Japan Society, Inc.

Lexington Books
D.C. Heath and Company
Lexington, Massachusetts
Toronto   London

Library of Congress Cataloging in Publication Data

Morley, James William, 1921-
   Prologue to the future.

   1. Japan—Social conditions—1945-   —Addresses, essays,
lectures. 2. Japan—Economic conditions—1945-   —Addresses,
essays, lectures. 3. United States—Social conditions—1960-
—Addresses, essays, lectures. 4. United States—Economic
conditions—1945-   —Addresses, essays, lectures. I. Frankel,
Charles, .1917-   II. Title.
HN727.M67   309.1'52'04   73-18491
ISBN 0-669-91751-6

Published simultaneously in Canada.

Printed in the United States of America.

International Standard Book Number: 0-669-91751-6

Library of Congress Catalog Card Number: 73:18491

Contents

List of Figure

and Tables

Foreword

　During November of 1972, four Japanese and four American specialists in economics, political science, sociology, communications, and philosophy gathered at Japan House at the invitation of the Japan Society to discuss and speculate on Japan and the United States as the world's first postindustrial societies on the threshold of what was termed "the informational revolution." Professor James William Morley of Columbia University, a director of the Japan Society, chaired the sessions and I served as conference coordinator. At the conclusion of their private discussions the group traveled to Wingspread, the conference center of The Johnson Foundation in Racine, Wisconsin, to share their views and findings with a wider audience. The papers presented on these occasions are brought together here to contribute to a greater public understanding of the age we Americans and Japanese recently have entered.

　As with all Society publications, this work represents solely the findings and views of the authors concerned, and should not be construed to reflect the views of Japan Society, Inc., its officers, directors, staff or members.

　A special word of thanks is due to The Johnson Foundation, without whose generosity this project would not have been possible; to the officers and directors of the Society, who provided leadership, understanding and encouragement; to the Society staff, which gave us the support we needed; and, most of all, to Professor Morley, whose friendship and guidance were unfailing and always available.

F. Roy Lockheimer
Associate Executive Director
Japan Society, Inc.

Part I
Introduction

Chapter One

The Futurists' Vision

James William Morley

In September 1968 an international symposium on the future
was held in Tokyo by the Japan Techno-Economics Society.
Intellectuals from all over the world gathered there and
marvelled at the future that science seemed to have un-
locked. The Japanese were riding the euphoria generated by
the phenomenal growth of their economy in the sixties. As
for the Americans, Nicholas Johnson, then a U.S. federal
communications commissioner, declared that success in the
space program had "impressed upon us the realization that
we have the human talent and economic resources to do
anything worth doing. . . . We are in the anomalous position of having capabilities that exceed our aspirations."[1]

The reason for this extraordinarily favorable state of
affairs was alleged to be that the industrial order was passing
and with it, the age-old problems of poverty, disease, and
human isolation were soon to become things of the past. We
in the "advanced societies," it was said, were about to
enter—indeed, already had begun to enter—a marvelous
new stage of history in which not labor and capital, but
information and intelligence were to play the key role in
production, and the educated man would be the focus of
social life and the vessel of leadership.

But even as the conferees were speaking, in the United

Written in early 1973

3

States the very citadels of the much-heralded knowledge explosion, the universities, were being overwhelmed by an unprecedented student revolt. Our cities were already seething with the discontent of the blacks and other minorities. Our economy was being throttled by recession; our politics were being embittered by the war in Indochina; and our very social fabric was being tugged out of shape by a new counter-culture. A sense of frustration and discontent was sweeping over the land, dividing our people between those demanding more change and those dug in to prevent it.

In Japan too, in spite of visions of unending economic prosperity and peace, the people were suffering from a revolt of the youth; a crisis in housing, transportation, health care, and the amenities of urban living; a pollution of the natural environment; and a shock to traditional values. They too were overtaken by problems belying the new promise.

Since then, Japan and the United States seem to have turned different corners. In America, the pall of the war in Indochina has been lifted, the economy rejuvenated, and the violence and emotionalism have begun to subside. The way might seem to be clear at last to turn to the promise of the future. But the truth is, certain problems of the past still plague us; and, in any event, the nation for the moment still has its head down. The mood in America is one of recuperation and retrenchment.

In Japan, by contrast, the most recent years have brought a heightened sense of competence and vigor. Peace and economic growth have been the dominant experiences; and with the reelection of the independent, Ryokichi Minobe, to the governorship of Tokyo in 1971, the recovery of the progressives in the general election of 1972, and the election of Kakuei Tanaka to the premiership earlier that year, a vibrant, optimistic, reformist spirit is coursing through the land.

This difference in current national mood between the United States and Japan, however, should not obscure the great interest that changes in one have for the other, for both are challenged by historically similar situations. Being among the most "advanced" societies, both face the problems and promises of the new era of postindustrialism which has been introduced by high technology, affluence, education, and urbanization. At the same time, older loyalties continue to attract large segments of their populations, and problems generated by the frictions of the past continue to plague them.

The consciousness that parts of American and Japanese societies are entering a new age is quite recent. To be sure, as the industrial revolution advanced, generating a steady growth in the output of goods and services, the conception began to take shape that ultimately a stage of high industrialization would be achieved when, to use the phrase in the Japanese Constitution, at least "the minimum standards of wholesome and cultured living" could be assured to all. Karl Marx thought that it would take a revolution in class relations and the triumph of socialism before such an equitable distribution could be achieved. John Maynard Keynes thought that "the economic problem," as he called it, might be solved simply by compounding the gains in production, but not for another hundred years.[2]

In 1958 W. W. Rostow gave a significant new twist to this older social theorizing.[3] Reacting particularly against the deterministic and cataclysmic elements of Marx's thought and the conservatism of Keynes' forecast, he proposed a new theory of the stages of development. All economically developing societies, he said, could be thought of as evolving by a series of stages from the relatively static condition of traditionalism, characterized by primitive agriculture, through "take-off" when the systematic application of new technology promised a steady increase in the society's economic output. This post-take-off stage corresponded in general to what had previously been called the age of industrialization. For Rostow, this age developed to the point of "maturity," when all of the society's resources were being exploited by the new technology. And this point, which he

5

judged America to have reached around 1900 and Japan in about 1940, was in turn the threshold to a higher stage, which he characterized as the "mass consumption society." By this he meant to suggest that by the postwar period, economic output in both Japan and the United States had become so plentiful that they no longer needed to devote themselves to expanding production but could concentrate on distributing to every man the goods and services he wanted. How soon this distribution problem would be solved in the United States, he was not sure since he foresaw a rise in America's population which might perpetuate scarcity for some time to come.

The population did not increase so significantly as Rostow expected. Indeed, the rate of GNP growth over the past decade in the United States has continued to outstrip it by a ratio of 3:1 and in Japan by the phenomenal ratio of 10:1. But the concepts of "take-off" and "maturity" proved to be too slippery to date confidently. In the case of Japan, E. Sydney Crawcour, for example, saw the preconditions for "take-off" being laid far back in the Tokugawa period;[4] and two other economic historians of Japan, Kazushi Ohkawa and Henry Rosovsky, demonstrated that in spite of a favorable production-population growth ratio, Japan could not be said to have reached Rostovian "maturity" even by the 1960s since the traditional sector of its economy had not yet been eliminated.[5] In any event, a continuing drive to expand production did not seem inconsistent with a simultaneous increase in mass consumerism as Japan's experience in the 1960s clearly demonstrated. A revision of Rostow's conception seemed called for.

At this point a new indicator of economic growth began to attract attention: the rise of the service sector. Some years before, A.G.B. Fisher and Colin Clark had formalized and quantified the idea that the economy might usefully be divided into primary, secondary, and tertiary sectors, the primary consisting of agriculture, the secondary of industry, and the tertiary of services.[6] They observed further that as

6

the income level rose, demand tended to shift from the primary to the secondary and then to the tertiary; and where demand called, production and the labor force seemed to follow.

But it was Daniel Bell who in the late 1960s saw the possibilities of using this insight for a much broader social analysis.[7] Correlating changes in the service sector with other salient developments in the economy and society at large, he became convinced that it was this shift in the economic structure which best explained the crisis in the "advanced" societies. What is happening to them, he observed, is that they are crossing the threshold from economies in which the secondary or industrial sector has taken most of the labor force and produced most of the goods and services (characteristic of the "industrial society" of the past) to economies in which the tertiary or service sector, that is, trade, transportation, finance, insurance, real estate, service, and government play this role. This, he argued, is a shift of vast importance, for it means that whereas the manual and the unskilled workers have been the basic force of the industrial society, it is the skilled, the educated, the "knowledge workers" who form the new service class; and it is to meet the needs of this class that the new "post-industrial" society will be shaped. The United States, he argued, is in the first stages of this postindustrial society and Japan is not far behind.

Herman Kahn, another futurist, seems generally to accept the notion of postindustrial society, but offers his own variant on it.[8] He prefers to stress an older indicator—the level of per capita income. He points out that until the last two or three centuries, no large human society had ever produced more than the equivalent of $200 per capita annually. The industrial revolution enabled man to break out of this pattern and thereafter, as his per capita income increased, to move by stages into a more and more affluent style of life, requiring at each stage the building of new social structures and the embracement of new values to corre-

7

spond. Agreeing with Rostow that a "mass consumption" stage represents the highest form of the "industrial" order, he suggests that a society may be recognized to have entered this stage when its per capita income reaches the $2,000 mark; and he suggests that when the per capita income climbs to the $4,000 level, it may be taken as an indication that the transition to a postindustrial order has begun.[9]

As may be seen from Table 1-1, these conceptions result in a quite different interpretation of American and Japanese experience from those of Rostow or Bell. Applying Kahn's criteria, we should have to conclude that the United States entered the mass consumption phase of industrialism in about 1951 and began what is probably a long transition to postindustrialism only in 1971. Japan, on the other hand, if we look only at its postwar history, did not reach an "industrial" level of per capita income until 1967, twenty-five years later than the United States. Then, as a result of its extraordinary rate of economic growth, it passed within five years (1972) into a mass consumption phase, from which, if its growth continues at this pace, it will begin the transition to postindustrialism sometime in the late 1970s.

But if historical eras are to have any meaning, can one suppose that any country has passed through them so quickly? There would seem to be a serious question about the applicability of Kahn's per capita income criteria to Japan. Bell's emphasis on the service sector as an indicator of the new age is more useful, but there are problems here too. What is the appropriate indicator of the importance of the service sector? If one takes the percentage of the work force engaged in that sector, one finds as shown in Table 1-2 that roughly 50 percent of the work force became engaged in the service sector in the United States in the early 1950s and in Japan will become so engaged probably this year. This accords roughly with Bell's conception that America has recently entered and Japan will soon enter the postindustrial age. But if one takes the percentage of the GNP produced by the service sector, Bell's timing is somewhat confuted. As

8

Table 1-1
Kahn's Era Indicators Applied to the United States and Japan[a]

Era	Threshold Per Capita Income (in Current $)	Year the Era Began for U.S.[b]	Year the Era Began for Japan[c]
Preindustrial ———————			
Early industrial	300	c. 1910	1959
Industrial	1,000	1942	1967
Mass consumption	2,000	1951	1972
Emerging postindustrial	4,000	1971	
Postindustrial	10,000		

[a]Era names and threshold amounts are taken from "Synoptic Context One: The Prospects for Mankind and a Year 2000 Ideology, Draft," (Croton-on-Hudson: Hudson Institute, August 1, 1972), an unpublished paper cited by permission, p. 22.

[b]Data to 1957 and derived from U.S. Bureau of the Census, *Historical Statistics of the United States. Colonial Times to 1957* (Washington, D.C., 1960), pp. 7 and 139; later data from U.S. Bureau of the Census, *Statistical Abstract of the United States, 1972* (Washington, D.C., 1972), pp. 5 and 317.

[c]Derived from Nihon Seisansei Honbu, *Katsuyō rōdō tōkei (1972 nenpan)* [Useful Labor Statistics, 1972] (Tokyo 1972), p. 29; and Bureau of Statistics, *Monthly Statistics of Japan*, no. 135 (September 1972), pp. 3 and 122. Yen figures for 1959 and 1967 were converted at the then prevailing rate of 360 yen = $1.00; the 1972 yen figure was converted at the revalued rate of 308 yen = $1.00.

shown in Table 1-3, Japan's service sector began to account for more than half the GNP about ten years ago. In the United States, on the other hand, service has been the leading sector for a very considerable period of time. As long ago as 1930, for example, the service sector accounted for more than 60 percent of the GNP; in succeeding years it first declined in share, then recovered to about that same level by 1960.[10] Why this should be would need lengthier analysis than is possible here, but it seems reasonable to suppose that the size and relative growth of the various sectors depend on the country's comparative advantage as well as on its per capita income.[11] Lebanon, for example, has probably the highest percentage of its labor force (two-thirds) in the service sector of any country in the world, but it is not usually considered to be the most "advanced" society in the world.

Beyond these issues, there is the broader structural

Table 1-2

Percentage Distribution of Employed Persons by Economic Sector in the United States and Japan

				Agriculture	Industry[a]	Service[b]
	U.S.[c]	Japan[d]	U.S.[e]	Japan[d]	U.S.[e]	Japan[d]
1955	10.4%	41.2%	36.2%	24.4%	53.4%	34.4%
1960	8.3	33.4	34.5	28.2	57.2	38.4
1965	6.1	24.3	33.7	32.8	60.2	42.8
1970	4.5	16.5	31.7	35.7	63.8	47.3

[a]Industry includes manufacturing, construction, and mining.

[b]Service includes wholesale and retail trade, government, services, transportation, public utilities, finance, insurance, and real estate.

[c]Derived from data for employed civilian labor force in U.S. Bureau of the Census, *Statistical Abstract of the United States, 1970* (Washington, D.C., 1970), p. 213.

[d]Derived from data in *Monthly Statistics of Japan*, no. 1, p. 8; and no. 26, p.8.

[e]Since the U.S. official data for "nonagricultural establishments" in *Statistical Abstract*, p. 218, excludes certain categories of workers who are included in the totals for nonagricultural employees in the civilian labor force, ibid., p. 213, the arbitrary assumption is made here that those so excluded from the former table would be distributed in the industrial and service sectors in approximately the same proportions as those included. Accordingly, the percentages for industrial and service sectors derived from the data ibid., p. 218, were applied to the total percentages for nonagricultural employment derived from the data ibid., p. 213, to produce the figures above. This is admittedly a crude procedure, but consistent data are not readily available.

issue: by concentrating attention on certain "advanced" parts of society, each of these theories tends to ignore the less advanced parts, downplaying the coexistence within any complex culture of its many subcultures. Zbigniew Brzezinski, for example, suggests that there exist today "three Americas in one."[12] There is the "technetronic America" (his word for the emerging postindustrial society) of the scientist and the technician; the "industrial America" of the blue-collar worker; and the "preindustrial America" of the sharecropper and the migrant, who have not yet experienced the industrial revolution, let alone the transition to the age beyond. And the observer of the Japanese scene cannot help but recognize the validity of Ohkawa's and

Table 1-3

Percentage Distribution of GNP by Economic Sector: United States and Japan[a]

	U.S.[e]	Japan[f]	U.S.[e]	Agriculture[b] Japan[f]	Industry[c] U.S.[e]	Service[d] Japan[f]
1955	8.1%	22.7%	35.9%	28.9%	56.0%	48.1%
1960	6.8	14.6	33.2	36.5	60.0	49.1
1965	5.7	11.2	33.6	35.9	60.7	53.3
1970	4.9	7.5	30.7	38.0	64.4	54.7

[a] At current prices.

[b] Includes agriculture, forestry, fishery, and mining.

[c] Includes manufacturing and construction.

[d] Includes trade, finance, insurance, real estate, transportation, communications, public utilities, services, and government.

[e] Derived from data in U.S. Bureau of the Census, *Historical Statistics of the United States. Colonial Times to 1957* (Washington, D.C., 1960), p. 140.

[f] Nihon Seisansei Honbu, *Katsu yo rodo tokei (1972) nenpan)* [Useful labor statistics, 1972] (Tokyo 1972), p. 34.

Rosovsky's observation already referred to, that elements of the traditional economy, for example, on farms and in household shops, persist side-by-side with the most modern of industrial establishments, as well as the television studios of postindustrialization.

These reservations are meant not to deny the futurists' vision, but to qualify it. For if the totality of the advancing societies is too complex to be embraced in the single rubric of "postindustrial," a significant and growing segment of each society can certainly be so identified; and if no single indicator seems satisfactory for dating the time when postindustrial forces first begin to assert themselves in the United States and Japan, we cannot fail to recognize that the influence of these forces is increasingly being felt. Incomes in Japan and America are clearly setting new records. New technologies are revolutionizing the communications and other service industries. Knowledge is expanding; higher

11

education is becoming the birthright of the masses. And these developments are creating for each society a similar set of new problems. Each needs to find, for example, new patterns of urban living, new structures for creating and disseminating knowledge, and new values to guide the changing relations between the generations and the sexes. Taken together, such trends and problems constitute a cluster of social issues which, for their importance and their novelty, may usefully be recognized as future-oriented or postindustrial.

On the other hand, even the most "advanced" societies have their industrial and preindustrial sectors. Significant groups of Americans and Japanese still engage in agriculture and much larger groups are working in industry. Moreover, it is clear to anyone touring the American Appalachian region or the Japanese Tohoku area that the isolation and poverty which characterize traditional agriculture have not yet been wholly eliminated, nor has the threat of seasonal or technological unemployment been driven from the factory town. The past lives on and its problems are as urgent as those of the future.

A reservation must also be made to the futurists' implication of the convergence of our two societies. This implication stems from a too simplistic assumption of single-factor determinism: that there is a single "key" to a society and that as its technology, its income, or its economic structure goes, so go its politics and its art. To be sure, politics and art as well as many other aspects of a society are often profoundly influenced by changes in its economic structure or its technological skills, but the currents of influence do not flow in one direction only. The search for "the key" which unlocks all the secrets of society, whether it be in economic development or technological change, is as futile as the search of Ponce de Leon for the fountain of youth.

This becomes clear when one appreciates the striking degree of autonomy of political and cultural affairs. Recently the idea of economic development has been so persuasive

12

that more and more political scientists have begun to look at the polity also in developmental terms. It has become customary to speak of certain states, like India or Nigeria, as "developing," meaning that their "traditional" political systems are undergoing significant "modernization," and to designate states like Japan and the United States as "developed" or "advanced," indicating that they have arrived or have nearly arrived at their "modern" transformation. The exact political content of these rubrics has been difficult to define though it usually includes such elements, for example, as the extent of nationalist sentiment, bureaucratic rationalization, political participation, and centralized planning.[13] It is easy to see that the increase in such elements has tended to grow as certain states have become more industrially "mature." It has not been possible, however, to demonstrate across-the-board causation. Moreover, it is impossible to deny the persistence of many elements of the polity which seem to have a life of their own. These elements are influenced by their environment, to be sure, but they seem to be able to coexist with a variety of economic stages and to therefore enjoy a relative autonomy. The monarchical institution in Japan, for example, founded in ancient times, has survived the onslaught of industrialism and seems, at the present moment at least, in no danger of falling victim to the computers, the television sets, or the service workers of the tertiary sector. The American presidency seems similarly resilient.

Nor is the cultural aspect the obvious creature of technology and economics. It is influenced, to be sure: television has replaced the movie as the standard form of mass entertainment, but the movie form has not died. "Hippie" values appeal to some youth, but "square" values continue to appeal to others. One might attempt to explain the coexistence of such cultural configurations by suggesting their dependence on corresponding subsystems of economics or technology. To a certain extent this would appear to be true, but beyond this, one must recognize that a culture too has a considerable life of its own. It is out of the warp of a nation's own past concepts, art forms, values and tastes as well as the woof of contemporary life, whether experienced directly or borrowed from abroad, that it weaves its living culture. The Buddhist-Confucianist tradition in Japan is at least equally as important as the factory or the television studio in the formation of Japan's contemporary culture, just as the Judaeo-Christian tradition and eighteenth-century rationalism continue significantly to shape American culture.

In characterizing a society, therefore, one must be sensitive not just to those phases which seem influenced by the changing economy or technology but also to the relative autonomy of the polity and the culture and to the national differences in the "traditions" involved. The structures and values that survive from other economic eras in Japan are not synonomous with those that persist in the United States. To give a few examples, it has long been recognized that the individualism that is so highly prized in the United States, is a far less important value in Japan than cooperation with and, in the end, conformity to the group. Authority is more deferred to in Japan than in the United States, and the bureaucracy more powerful. Japanese prefer consensual modes of decision-making to the majoritarian style of Americans. In a different area of life, the Japanese culture is more emotional, more expressive than ours, at the same time that it is more patterned.

No doubt, in the long run as the industrial and postindustrial forces increase their influence, our two societies will become increasingly alike. Accordingly, it will be increasingly useful to work together to solve our common emerging problems.

But certainly in our time and for the foreseeable future the convergence of our societies will be imperfect. The relatively homogeneous Japanese people's two-thousand years of experience in their beautiful, but poorly endowed and isolated archipelago will continue to create certain problems and sustain certain preferences which are different from those of the Americans, whose relatively short, primary experience has been the subduing of a rich continent. The persistence of a depressed sector of nonmechanized industry, for example, is of unique concern to Japan while the problem of the black man is peculiar to America. Even postindustrial problems like environmental pollution and urban congestion, which plague both our societies, arise in different social and political contexts.

We have much to learn from each other in how to cope with both our unique and our common problems, but in the end each of our societies must find its own path to the future, making its own decisions in response to the peculiar conditions, institutions, and values which continue to shape its separate life. These differences, too, we must learn to understand and value, for it is variety that gives life its savor.

Notes

1. Nicholas Johnson, "Communications and the Year 2000," a paper presented at the binational conference on "Perspectives on Post-Industrial Society," held ln Tokyo, September 25-27, 1968 (mimeo), p. 16.

2. J. M. Keynes, "Economic Possibilities for our Grandchildren," written in 1930 and reprinted in *Essays in Persuasion,* as cited in Herman Kahn, "Synoptic Context One: The Prospects for Mankind and a Year 2000 Ideology" (Croton-on-Hudson: Hudson Institute, August 1, 1972), pp. 24-25.

3. In a lecture subsequently published in *The Stages of Economic Growth* (Cambridge: Cambridge University Press, 1961).

4. E. Sydney Crawcour, "The Tokugawa Heritage," in William W. Lockwood, ed., *The State and Economic Enterprise in Japan* (Princeton: Princeton University Press, 1965), pp. 17-46.

15

5. Kazushi Ohkawa and Henry Rosovsky, "A Century of Japanese Economic Growth," in Lockwood, *State and Economic Enterprise in Japan,* pp. 47-92.

6. For example, in A. G. B. Fisher, *The Clash of Progress and Security* (London: Macmillan, 1935) and Colin Clark, *Conditions of Economic Progress,* 3rd. ed. London: Macmillan, 1957), both cited in Everett E. Hagen, *The Economics of Development* (Homewood, Illinois: Richard D. Irwin, 1968), p. 45. Hollis Chenery, Simon Kuznets, and others have developed these theme further.

7. Daniel Bell, "The Measurement of Knowledge and Technology," in Eleanor Sheldon and Wilbert Moore, eds., *Indicators of Social Change* (Russell Sage Foundation: New York, 1969), and more recently in "Technocracy and Politics," in *Survey* (Winter 1971), pp. 1-24.

8. See for example, Herman Kahn and Anthony J. Wiener, "The Next Thirty-Three Years: A Framework for Speculation," in Daniel Bell, ed., *Toward the Year 2000: Work in Progress* (Boston: Houghton Mifflin, 1968), pp. 73-100.

9. "Synoptic Context One: The Prospects for Mankind and a Year 2000 Ideology Draft" (Croton-on-Hudson: Hudson Institute, August 1, 1972), p. 22. An unpublished paper cited by permission. These threshold figures are a slight revision of those suggested earlier in Kahn and Wiener, "The Next Thirty-Three Years."

10. Data for 1930 derived from national income figures on U.S. Bureau of the Census, *Historical Statistics of the United States: Colonial Times to 1957* (Washington D.C., 1960), p. 140.

11. Hagen, *Economics of Development,* p. 48.

12. Zbigniew Brzezinski, *Between Two Ages: America's Role in the Technetronic Era* (New York: Viking, 1970), p. 200.

13. For a significant trait list, see Robert E. Ward, "Introduction," to his *Political Development in Modern Japan* (Princeton: Princeton University Press, 1969), pp. 3-9.

Part II
The Economy

Chapter Two

Economic Problems of a Postindustrial Society

Robert L. Heilbroner

The idea that we are moving rapidly into a "postindustrial" age with socioeconomic relationships sufficiently different from those of the recent past to warrant designation as a new "stage" of our historical development, needs to be treated somewhat skeptically. I do not quarrel with the argument that deep-seated changes in structure, institutions, and behavior are indeed surfacing within the economic sphere, whence they spread out to affect social and political life,[1] but unfortunately a certain voguish quality has come to surround the word postindustrial by which we describe this phenomenon.[2] Accordingly, it may be helpful to commence by specifying as clearly as possible what we mean by the postindustrial transformation, both to clarify its relationship to the "industrial" era now presumably on the wane, and to highlight those aspects of the coming era that are genuinely new.

Let me therefore start by exploring rather skeptically three different meanings that are commonly advanced with regard to the idea of a postindustrial society:

1. *A postindustrial society is one in which a preponderance of economic activity is located in the "tertiary" sector of the economy.*

This definition of postindustrialism calls attention to the shift in occupational locus whose beginnings can be discerned far back in the nineteenth century.[3] As the history of every industrialized country indicates, the proportion of the labor force employed in agriculture shrinks to a very small fraction of the total work force: in the United States only 4 percent of the civilian labor force is to be found on the farm and this includes a considerable residue of subsistence farmers. Meanwhile, the industrial "core," comprising manufacturing, mining, transportation, construction and utilities, has stabilized at roughly a third of the work force.[4] The remainder of the population—over 60 percent of the work force in the United States today—is employed in that congeries of occupations that produce "final" services.

From industrial nation to industrial nation the magnitude of these proportions varies, but the "drift" is visible in all (see Table 2-1).

Thus the definition of a postindustrial society that rests on a marked shift in the locus of employments can be amply demonstrated by statistical data. Nonetheless, a few cautionary remarks are in order. First, let us note that the industrial sector has not been the source of the main change in the profile of sectoral employment. Although it has declined slightly in France and England during the last twenty years, in Germany the percentage is unchanged; and in the United States *over a period of seventy years* the decline has been miniscule. The great sectoral tranformation of our times, in other words, has not been so much a shift from "industry" to "service" as a shift from agricultural to service tasks.[5]

In addition, we must note that some part of the rise in

Table 2-1
Percentage Distribution of Employed Workers in Selected Western Countries

	Agriculture	Industry	Service
U.S., 1900	38%	38%	24%
1970	4	35	61
France, 1950	35	45	20
1970	17	39	44
West Germany, 1950	24	48	28
1968	10	48	42
U.K., 1950	6	56	39
1970	4	45	50

Sources: U.S.: *Historical Statistics*, p. 74; *Economic Indicators* (1972)
European countries: OECD, *Basis Statistics of the Community* (1970)

service employment represents the transfer of certain kinds of work from the nonmonetized household sector to the monetized commercial world. The well-known rise in female labor participation (from 18 percent of all females of working age to 37 percent, in the years 1890 to 1969 in the United States) has brought as a consequence the illusion of a rise in service "employment," as tasks that were formerly carried out within the home, where they remained invisible to the eye of the statistician, emerged onto the marketplace. The growth of the laundry industry, the restaurant industry, the professional care of the aged, even "welfare," represents instances of this semispurious inflation of the growth of "employment" in service occupations.

These caveats and distinctions are important to bear in mind when we use the shift in employment locus as the basis for speculations about the implications of the postindustrial era. Let me briefly summarize what these cautionary thoughts might be.

Presumably, the importance of the employment shift for a postindustrial system is that a change in occupational habitat brings new social experiences and needs. Without in any way challenging that supposition, let me warn against the misconception of that change as a massive emigration from industrial work. Nothing of that kind is visible. Instead, the primary "experiential" fact of the employment shift has been the decisive decline of agricultural (farm) employment and a corresponding growth of market-located, service-connected tasks. The industrial "core" remains roughly constant. Put differently, the industrial factory worker—the key *dramatis persona* of the Marxian drama—continues to account for approximately the same proportion of the total work experience of the community: unskilled, semiskilled and skilled workers—the blue-collar group—constituted 25.5 percent of the labor force in 1900 and 34.9 percent in 1968, the main shift taking place *within* this group as most unskilled labor rose to semiskilled levels. Thus, if postindustrial society in fact represents a new stage of socioeconomic relationships, the cause must be sought elsewhere than in any disappearance of the industrial sector as a milieu for work.

2. *A postindustrial society may refer to a change in the nature of growth-producing inputs from quantitative to qualitative factors.*

Here the primary meaning of "postindustrial" calls our attention to numerous studies of growth within industrial countries, and to the more or less common conclusions that "knowledge" has played a steadily rising role in promoting growth, compared with increases in the size of the labor force or the quantity of (unchanged) capital.[6] Drawing on Denison's work, we may generalize for the United States that for the two decades prior to 1929 increases in the stock of capital goods and in labor supply together accounted for about two-thirds of our increase in output, whereas in the decades 1929-1959 increases in these quantitative factors accounted for only 44 percent of growth. Conversely, improved education and training, which were credited with only 13 percent of growth in the earlier period, were presumed to be the source of more than twice that proportion of growth in the later period. Finally, improved technology

—which is, after all, only the concrete application of knowledge—rose from 12 percent of the causes of growth to 20 percent in the same two periods.[7]

These proportions also differ from nation to nation, as Denison has shown in a study of the sources of growth in Western European nations, but the direction of change—as in the case of the migration of labor—is the same throughout. In sum, there is little doubt that statistical examination of growth patterns among industrialized nations shows a steadily increasing importance of "knowledge-related" inputs, and a corresponding decline in increases in brute "labor power" or sheer quantities of unchanged capital (for example, the addition of more railroad tracks).

As in the case of the definition of postindustrialism that emphasizes the shift in the locus of employment, I do not want to denigrate the importance that has been attached to human "capital."[8] Nonetheless it is important, as before, that we scrutinize this characterization of postindustrialism with a certain reserve. For when we do so, we encounter some disconcerting considerations.

First, as we have all come to realize, the meaning of growth is both ill-specified and elusive. Between that collection of often arbitrarily defined outputs called gross national product and any operational concept of welfare is a wide and perhaps unbridgeable chasm. Hence much of the "growth" to which modern knowledge seems to contribute so strikingly may be of little or no welfare significance: armaments, space exploration, and pollution-generating production at one extreme; frivolous gadgetry, style-changes, and pollution-absorbing technology at the other—the one extreme producing deleterious or dangerous growth, the other illusory or "defensive" growth. In a word, the *quality* of the growth of a postindustrial society must be compared with that of an industrial society before we can discuss the rise of knowledge-inputs as a cause for celebration, as well as a simple fact.

Second, before looking for the implications of the shift

25

toward a knowledge-input economy, it behooves us to in quire further into the "fact" of the increase in knowledge input itself. This brings us to the ways in which knowledge input is *measured*. One of these ways—research and development—is certainly grossly inflated. Government statistics show a rise in research and development expenditures from roughly $1 billion at the end of World War I to a level of $28 billion in the early 1970s. This enormous increase has led many observers to conclude that we have now "institutionalized" the process of scientific discovery and application, thereby radically changing the nature of the propulsive forces within the economy. More skeptical observers have noted that (inflation aside) the Research and Development figures in the later years are swollen by the growing tendency to include routine testing or marketing procedures within the category of "research." The actual amount going for basic research in new industrial products for 1966 was estimated to be not $20 billion, but $1 billion.[9]

In addition, a study by Jewkes, Sawers, and Stillerman throws considerable doubt on the effectiveness of "institutional" invention, citing evidence that the preponderance of the important inventions or innovations of the last third century have been made by individuals or small firms.[10] Thus there is some reason to regard the institutionalized knowledge-input of the postindustrial society as much less sharply differentiated from that of industrial society than might at first appear.

A further caveat with respect to the supposed information revolution applies to the rise in the "stock" of education embodied in the work force. Measured by the conventional criteria of man-years of schooling, there is no doubt that this stock has increased markedly: whereas only 6 percent of the population aged 17 were high school graduates in 1900, nearly 80 percent had completed high school in 1970. Equally dramatic, whereas those enrolled in college in 1900 constituted only 4 percent of the population aged 18-21, today well over half of this age group is in college.

26

No one can gainsay this change which, like the change in the sectoral location of labor, surely augurs new outlooks, experiences, and expectations on the part of the labor force. To this matter we will return. But it would be hasty to jump from the fact of a higher stock of embodied education to the conclusion that the stock of "knowledge" of the society has increased *pari passu*. For along with the increased training undergone by the labor force has come an increase in the compartmentalization and specialization of its skills, best exemplified by comparing the wide-ranging capabilities of the farmer with the much more narrowly defined work capabilities of the office clerk. To put the matter differently, we cannot assume that a postindustrial society is one in which the general level of "know-how" is raised along with the general level of formal education. Insofar as formal education is devoted to exposing the student to the broadest vistas of history, the social and natural sciences, and so forth, one kind of "knowledge" is undoubtedly increased. In that sense, the average citizen of the postindustrial society is not only "better educated" but really knows more, with regard to the natural sciences, human behavior, and so forth, *considered as abstractions,* than did his counterpart in industrial or preindustrial society. At a less abstract level, however, the gain is much less. And within that very important branch of social knowledge concerned with the operation of the socioeconomic mechanism, what seems to mark the education-intensive postindustrial society is a marked *decrease* in the ability of the individual to perform work outside his trained specialty—witness our helplessness in the face of a broken utensil, vehicle, electrical system or plumbing fixture, compared with the versatility of the farmer (or industrial artisan), proverbially jack of all trades, even if master of none.

To raise these cautions against a simplistic view of the postindustrial society as one characterized by a "knowledge explosion" is not to deny that profound alterations are visible within contemporary society as a result of greater educational inputs—alterations that are likely to become even more pronounced in the society of the future. The first of these, whose implications we will examine again subsequently, is a change in the expected lifestyles of a postindustrial population. Whatever else its effects may be, the exposure to prolonged schooling seems to encourage an expectation of careers in white-collar, as opposed to blue-collar tasks; and may indeed militate against the willingness of the "educated" population to consider many manual tasks as appropriate ways of making a livelihood, regardless of the relative incomes to be had from goods-handling, rather than paper-handling, work. Needless to say, this change in expectations accords very well with the actual displacement of labor from agricultural tasks and from the unskilled categories of industrial work, and its increasing deployment in service occupations.

Second and perhaps more important—although necessarily more conjectural—is the educationally based evolution of a "subclass" of highly skilled technicians, scientists, and experts who seem to be moving gradually toward a position of greater influence within the socioeconomic system as a whole. The rise of this "knowledge elite" has been remarked by many.[11] The actual power possessed by the new elite, as well as its degree of sub- or superordination to older elites, is as yet unclear. Nonetheless, there seems little doubt that a new education-based stratification has been created at the apex of the system, and that a new mystique surrounds "the scientist," symbol of the knowledge-oriented, postindustrial system, comparable to that which formerly adhered to the "captain of industry."[12] Thus the emphasis on "knowledge" as the *differentia specifica* of a postindustrial system is not misplaced, although the precise nature of this difference requires it to be spelled out a good deal more carefully than is often the case.

3. *A postindustrial society can be regarded as a "post-capitalist" society–that is, as a socioeconomic formation in which the traditional problems of capitalism will give way*

before the new organizational modes of a postindustrial system.

As with the previous "visions" of a postindustrial system, I think there is a core of truth in this view. The bitter class divisions endemic to capitalism in the late nineteenth and early twentieth centuries seem to be yielding to a society of much greater economic (if not necessarily social or political) consensus. The "welfare" state, however inadequate in actuality, is now a generally accepted model for all industrial societies, and brings with it a considerable degree of "socialism" in the form of guaranteed incomes, family allowances, public health assurance, educational subsidization of lower-income groups, and the like. The extreme vulnerability of the system to failures of aggregate demand has been tempered by the growth of a public sector. As a result of these and still other changes, the "revolutionary" proletariat has failed to materialize; moreover, as we have seen above, the size of the industrial proletariat has remained approximately constant.

Thus there *are* cogent reasons for thinking of the postindustrial society as one that differs in significant ways from the economic performance of the industrial capitalism to which it is a successor. Nonetheless, as before, it is wise to look for continuities as well as differences in seeking to delineate the nature of the new socioeconomic environment.

The first of these is the continuance of a trend whose origins can be traced back at least to the third quarter of the nineteenth century. This is the slow, irregular, but apparently irreversible trend toward the concentration of capital. The figures are well known: in manufacturing, the assets of the top 100 firms in 1968 were as large a share (roughly 49 percent) of all corporate manufacturing assets as the share of the 200 largest industrial firms in 1950. Similarly the top 200 firms in 1968 controlled as large a fraction of total assets as the top 1,000 firms in 1941.[13] Economic society today is strikingly characterized by what Robert Averitt has called a *center*—a small number of very large and powerful industrial

29

units—and a *periphery*—a very large number of generally small and weak firms.[14]

It should be noted that we are far from understanding the dynamics of this two-sector division with regard to the performance of the system as a whole. The oligopolistic center has been shown to be the source of much economic inefficiency and perhaps of inflationary pressures;[15] the sprawling periphery has been identified by at least one student as the main source of business instability.[16] More important, but even less well understood, are the extent and nature of the linkages that bind the center and political power structure. That linkages exist has been amply demonstrated, but the direction in which power flows (*from* the economic *to* the political structure, or vice versa) is unclear or perhaps unstable.[17] That is not a problem for this paper. Rather what I wish to stress is the existence of an economic concentrate allied in some fashion with a political concentrate—a state of affairs that is not basically different from that which existed under "industrial" society, and which can, incidentally, be seen as well in the economic-political ententes of Japan, France, Germany, and other candidates for entry into the postindustrial realm.[18]

The development of a postindustrial configuration of employment or education does not seem likely to undo this characteristic of economic concentration. Rather, it seems probable that the concentration process will now proceed rapidly in the burgeoning service sector, where significant inroads have already been made (as is also the case in agriculture, still by far the least concentrated sector). We tend to picture the service sector as comprised of large numbers of independent proprietorships (lawyers, self-employed, one-man enterprises); but in fact a considerable proportion of employment in this sector is already provided by monopolistic or oligopolistic units. Of roughly 44 millions employed in the service sector in 1970 (not including utilities or transportation), 13 millions were in government; 15 millions in trade, 4 millions in finance (banking, insurance,

30

brokerage, real estate). By comparison with the manufacturing sector, these are all relatively unconcentrated industries, but in terms of *absolute size of units,* the large firm, with its bureaucratic organization, is increasingly evident. A mere twenty-nine retail chains, for instance, control a fifth of all assets in trade. Similarly, the predominance and growth of large banks and insurance companies is well known: the top fifty banks account for a third of all banking employment; the top fifty insurance companies for almost half of all employment in that field. *Thus the organizational character of industrial capitalism with its hierarchies, bureaucracies, and above all, its trend toward concentration, seems likely to continue in the postindustrial society.*

Next, we find the distribution of wealth and income little if at all disturbed by the types of changes we have discussed. Many studies[19] have shown the extraordinary stability of income shares accruing to the top and bottom deciles in the United States; the top 10 percent of family units receiving about 30 percent of income, the bottom 30 percent less than 10 percent of income. These shares have remained roughly constant or have inclined slightly toward inequality during the late decade, in which the effects of the postindustrial changes might have been expected to reveal their influence.

More significant is the stubborn continuation and defense of the extreme concentration of wealth in the top 1 or 2 percent of family units who collectively own about a third of *all* wealth. Control of corporate wealth—by far the most strategic item of wealth—is much more tightly centered, with about two-thirds of such wealth in the hands of 0.2 percent of all families.[20] In passing, it might be remarked that this extreme concentration of control is not peculiar to capitalism—it could no doubt be found under feudalism and (insofar as power can be used as a proxy for wealth) under existing forms of socialism. What is specifically capitalist about the phenomenon is the focus of control on corporate enterprise; and there is no sign that this concentration or its focus will diminish appreciably in a postindustrial setting,

31

although the wealth-holding elites may recruit new-comers from the scientific-technological community.

Finally, we pass from structure to function. We have already noted that the more extreme destabilizing tendencies of capitalism now seem to be faced with rough-and-ready remedies. Let us only add that the specific features of post-industrialism that we have heretofore discussed—the sectoral shift and the increased education input—are not in themselves the source of any stabilizing tendencies (although one might claim that the defensive weaponry of macroeconomics is itself in part a product of the knowledge input of our time). However successfully we may have obviated the threat of mass unemployment and catastrophic income decline, there is scant evidence as yet that postindustrial society has solved problems that reflect the capitalist *modus operandi*. Inflation has replaced deflation, but the one, like the other, is surely a market phenomenon. A massive misallocation of resources, visible especially in the decay of the cities, has taken public priority over mass unemployment; but once again the fault lies with the failure of the market mechanism and the special constraints of private ownership. Specifically "capitalist" relations with the underdeveloped world seem to have worsened in the most recent period, or perhaps we should simply say that the capitalist problem of "imperialism" has reemerged to a central position.

All these elements suggest that whatever else we may say about the postindustrial future, *we should consider it as a stage of capitalism and not as a step "beyond" capitalism.* The stage may display new endemic characteristics and problems—indeed, I shall next turn to an exploration of what these may be—but it must also be expected to manifest many of the structural attributes of industrial capitalism, including concentrated economic power and wealth, a highly unequal distribution of pre- (and probably post-) tax income, and macro-malfunctions and misallocations of resources that arise from the predominance of the market as the principal allocatory mechanism.

Shall we then dismiss the idea of a postindustrial society as a chimera? That is not my intention. Just as late industrial capitalism differs in striking and significant ways from the small-scale capitalism of Adam Smith's day, so it is probable that the postindustrial trends within contemporary capitalism are pushing in directions that also portend substantial change.

Let me therefore turn the coin over and review the evidence I have just marshalled in order to factor out those elements that seem to me particularly freighted with change. The first of these, we will remember, had to do with the sectoral relocation of the work force away from the farm through the factory and into the office. Is it possible to generalize about the effects of such a massive relocation, particularly when one takes into account the extraordinary heterogeneity of tasks contained within the service sector?[21]

One such generalization is self-evident, but none the easier to interpret. It is a far-reaching change in the character of what we call, or think of, as "work." Like industrial man, postindustrial man is divorced from knowledge of the most fundamental provisioning activities of society: the seasons affect him only insofar as they determine his vacation time, the weather only as it upsets his travel plans or conditions his choice of clothing. Unlike industrial man, however, who also shares in this complete ignorance of the fundamental provisioning tasks, postindustrial man is no longer even familiar with the environment in which the great bulk of our industrial products originate. The bleak expanse of the factory wasteland, surrounded with its high, electrified fence; the clangor of the industrial shed, the dirty work clothes, the lunch pail, the grease, the grime, the dust that we find in most places of industrial work are missing from the store and the office. Changed too, is the character of work supervision, away from factory whistles, check-ins, foremen. Service work, in all or most of its varieties is characterized by trim surroundings, neat dress or a prestigious uniform, constant exposure

33

to a "clientele," coffee breaks, telephone calls. This is by no means all gain, although some of it is. The physical dangers of work are less; the psychological strains may be greater. The expenditure of physical effort is greatly reduced; that of psychic energies may be greatly increased.

It is difficult to know what conclusions follow from this impressionistically drawn change in work milieu. For example, whether "alienation" is exacerbated or alleviated is a matter about which we cannot even make informed guesses, not least because of the variety of tasks embraced within the service sector. Yet, in full awareness of the frailty of such "sociologizing," let me hazard one conjecture that combines the changed work experience mentioned above with a second characteristic of the postindustrial world—namely, the lengthened and broadened exposure of its work force to formal education. The conjecture (it is perhaps too untestable to be dignified with the name of "hypothesis"), is that the lengthened exposure to the "white-collar" atmosphere of the classroom tends to identify the expected characteristics of "work." That is, college prepares one not only intellectually, but experientially, for the store and the office rather than for the factory or the farm. I am aware, of course, of exceptions: agronomists, engineers, and a few similar professions. But in the main I think I am on firm ground in holding that education nurtures the association of "work" with reading, writing, and calculation, rather than with handling things. Thus the postindustrial society encourages what Veblen called a "trained incapacity" for "dirty work" among that ever-growing fraction of the population that pursues formal education through the college level. In passing, I should note that the smooth running of postindustrial society may hinge even more than that of industrial society, on the presence of that "secondary" labor force (the dropouts, casual labor-market participants, or exploited minorities) who continue to be available for the picking of fruit, the digging of ditches, the sweeping of floors, the washing of dishes.

Along with the new sense of what "work" means comes, I think, a growing expectation of security in the world of work. A man or woman who has been relieved of virtually all economic necessity until the age of twenty-one or even twenty-five is reared in an environment in which some sort of economic provision, even if at a frugal level, is taken for granted. It would not be surprising if the graduates of the postindustrial educational institutions bring with them strong expectations that "work" is not a scarce privilege to be competed for, but a basic right—the normal reward for having completed the long training that society has enjoined. Guarantees of employment, security of tenure in work, the "right" to expect an uninterrupted flow of income are thus plausible consequences of the transition to a postindustrial occupational and educational framework. Perhaps this is nothing more than the diffusion among the great bulk of the population of attitudes that were formerly evident mainly among the upper decile.

Let me turn finally to another new attribute of the postindustrial world which also follows from the characteristics we have examined in our previous section. This concerns the problems of economic function and malfunction that a postindustrial society can expect to inherit from its precursor.

Here one major trend seems likely to be reinforced by the postindustrial system. This is the growth of business-state coordination at an overt rather than covert level. Business-state cooperation is, of course, as old as capitalism itself; it is the mythology rather than the reality of laissez-faire which has dominated the past century. Many forces within the postindustrial framework seem likely to diminish the strength of that mythology and to strengthen the tendencies toward open coordination. The importance of maintaining an adequate level of aggregate demand in the face of widespread expectations of "guaranteed white-collar work," of remedying the disruptive effects of the misallocation of resources, and of dealing with the problems of an economic system increasingly polarized between a center and a periphery all seem likely to increase the need for, and the political accept-ability of, some kind of "planning." No doubt the form and functions of this planning will display differing reaches and effectiveness in various societies with their particular ideological, traditional, and structural differences, but in all postindustrial systems I would anticipate something that might be described as a "corporate state"—that is, a state in which the activities of the center and the state are brought into compatible paths, in which the risks and instabilities of the periphery are offset, or at least partially underwritten, and in which acceptable resource allocation is attacked by coordinated action between the public and private sectors.

In suggesting that the changeful elements of the postin-dustrial trend will encourage overt planning, I do not mean to imply that the politico-economic problems of this stage of capitalism will necessarily be easier to solve than those of industrial capitalism. The difficulties of controlling inflation may well be more recalcitrant than those of overcoming depression, both to diagnose and to cope with politically. The power of the moderately affluent middle classes, and of the service-sector located work force may prove more troublesome for a viable "incomes policy" than the wage-determination in an industrial setting (the recent experience in the municipal sectors as a case in point).[22] No less of a difficult problem for the macro management of the postin-dustrial system may be that of persuading the majority of income recipients, whose incomes lie in the fourth income decile and up, to relinquish substantial sums for the benefit of the poor who are to be found in the bottom three deciles. All these problems seem likely to add further impetus to the overall drift toward business-state planning to which we have already pointed.

Heretofore I have been discussing the postindustrial so-ciety from two points of view; first, analyzing the inade-quacies of certain views concerning the term; second, sug-gesting the kernel of truth that resides in these views. Now I wish to proceed in a somewhat different direction. First, I wish to inquire into two structural or transformational stresses to which postindustrial society will be subject, beyond those that we have already identified. Finally, I will ask the much more difficult question as to the social consequences we can anticipate as a consequence of these changes.

What further *economic* changes can be expected from the trajectory out of agrarian, through industrial, into the service-centered, education-intensive system we call "postindustrial"? Two such changes appear integrally connected with this trajectory, although as we shall see, the connections are not the same in each case.

The first change has to do with the progressive mechanization of work—that is, with the further development of the very force that lies behind the trajectory of economic transformation itself. There is no doubt that technology is the major element in bringing about the sectoral migration of the labor force, for it has been the widening "technicization" of rural and then factory work that has released the manpower that has flowed into the tertiary areas of the economy.[23] We do not fully understand the reason for the particular sequence of technology that has given us this shift and cannot therefore make firm predictions with respect to the future. But every indication is that invention and innovation will be proportionately more concentrated on the tasks performed in the service sector. This seems likely for three reasons: (1) we are reaching the limits of labor-displacement in agriculture (although there remains a small group that can still be dispossessed from their jobs in that sector); (2) almost three-quarters of a century of invention and innovation within the industrial core has left the proportion of the labor force relatively unchanged, as we have seen, and we can therefore assume that if the same general forces of technology and demand continue, there will not be significant labor displacement from this sector; and (3) the most "attractive" sector for the introduction of machinery lies in the heretofore technically "neglected" service area.[24] In this sector labor costs are high, productivity low, and a new level of technological capability begins to bring many heretofore "unmechanizable" tasks within the reach of machinery. As a result we have the vending machine for the counter man; the self-service store for the clerk; the programmed lathe, the automatic check-reader, the omnipresent computer.

What will be the effect of this further mechanization? The answer hinges entirely on the elasticity of demand for the services produced in this sector. If demand swells *pari passu* with the increased productivity per service worker that will result from "automation," then the service sector may continue to absorb its present 60-65 percent of the labor force. If demand swells more rapidly, or if technology enters more slowly, employment in this sector may rise still further in both absolute and percentage terms. It is also possible that the demand for "services," like that for "manufactures," will ultimately reach "satiety." In more concrete terms, there may be a limit as to the amount of government services, retail trade services, education, recreation, financial advice, and so forth, that a man wants at a given income level; and that the "amount" of services (measured in the dollars we spend for them) may not rise as rapidly as income rises.

In that case, where will the displaced labor go? Several possibilities for adjustment are available. One is the creation of a public employment sector designed to create employment for those displaced from the service area. This sector need not itself be within the tertiary sector, but might embrace subsidized small farming, labor-intensive subsidized handicraft, labor-intensive public construction, and so forth. A second possibility is the deliberate steady reduction in the work force, achieved partly by further extending the compulsory years of schooling, partly by reducing retirement ages, partly by shortening the work week. A third possibility is the extension of the transfer mechanism to permit a certain proportion of the young working-age population to live without work, at socially determined subsistence levels, if it so chooses.

All these adjustments—the need for which hinges, let me

38

repeat, on the unpredictable rate of technological displacement and the shift in the demand for various services —portend considerable strains on the "traditional" capitalist mechanism. They imply a high degree of that overall planning of which I spoke earlier. They imply as well new strains on the macro processes of a system in which the historic underpinning identified by both Marx and Weber—a propertyless class of workers—has been replaced by a class of workers which, however "propertyless," are not *forced* to sell their labor power at the prevailing market rate. It would be foolhardy to assert that an economic system operating under the constraints of "capitalist" ideologies and institutions cannot make these adjustments—one has but to consider the very great degree of social adaptation displayed by the capitalist nations of Scandinavia. But the basic nature of the challenge of mechanization is nonetheless clear. The postindustrial society is likely to be faced with a "redundancy" of labor owing to the progressive incursion of mechanization into the service sector; and this redundancy, if it is not absorbed by a spontaneous growth of private demand for "services," will require intervention into the market process on a far-reaching scale.

A second dimension of the mechanization problem has already engaged our attention. This is the effect of "automation" on the psycho-physical process of "work" itself. We have already seen that the displacement of "muscular" by "intellectual" labor is one of the main attributes of postindustrialization. Even at the simplest level—the man behind the tractor wheel instead of behind the hoe, behind the adding machine instead of behind the ledger, behind the computerized lathe instead of behind the chuck lathe—the nature of human effort in postindustrial society is given a supervisory, rather than directly "active," aspect. This change in the existential and experiential character of labor offers rich ground for speculation, but little substantial basis for extraeconomic prediction. We return at the conclusion of the chapter to this problem of social forecasting.

A second structural challenge to be faced by the postindustrial world is the problem of ecological adjustment that must be faced over the coming decades—a problem that will steadily grow in intensity as population densities rise, pollution accumulates, and resources become depleted.

The dimensions of the ecological problem are ultimately very great and its restrictive implications severe. What is at question is the time scale during which adjustment can be made and the degree of technological adaptation that can be achieved.[25] At stake is the level of qualitative well-being, the rate of tolerable growth, and in the end, the viability of the planet itself as a human habitat. It need hardly be said that the ecological threat affects not just the postindustrial world, but all nations, albeit in different fashions and at varying time schedules. In terms of the immediate impact on the quality of life, it may well be the most developed nations, with their high rate of pollution and their voracious consumption of resources, that stand to be the first affected.

When the ecological problem arrives "in earnest," it will pose an acute problem for postindustrial societies. We have already called attention to the presence, and the undoubted continuing importance, of the industrial core which, together with the agricultural sector, supports the tertiary activities of the postindustrial world. The problem, then, is the extent to which the expansive drive of a capitalist mechanism, expressed through the acquisitive and accumulatory behavior of its corporations, can be given an appropriate area in which to manifest itself, if unrestricted growth within the industrial sector becomes impermissible for environmental reasons.

Of the many new sources of tension and malfunction within the postindustrial world, this looming constriction of the expansive drive within the industrial sector seems among the most difficult of solution. The export of capital, a major means of venting the expansive drive in the past, becomes less open, due to environmental problems of pollution in the other developed countries (which are currently most attractive to capital), and to political problems in the underdeveloped world. To what extent the expansive international momentum of capitalism can be diverted to the areas of services is an uncertain question, but not one that seems especially promising, as the various "service" occupations are now defined.

There is no point in attempting to guess to what degree industrial companies will be able to move into such fields as entertainment, travel, personal services and the like. What is important to bear in mind is that some form of "growth," with all its money illusions and its mixture of "goods" and "bads," is an indispensable means of lessening the tensions generated by the need to divide the total product between wages and property income. In a postindustrial society in which industrial expansion were necessarily constrained because of ecological hazards, and in which the large corporation had not found a satisfactory means of penetrating the service occupations, we could expect serious stresses to manifest themselves—a fall in profit rates and/or a much more acrimonious struggle over the division of the social product. Whether "capitalism" could adjust to such a situation is moot—in the opinion of economists as different in orientation as Marx and Keynes it could not—but in all likelihood such a trend would accelerate the tendency toward the "managerialization" of the public-private corporate state to which other tendencies, discussed above, already point.

We have already indulged in sufficient speculation with regard to the socioeconomic characteristics of the postindustrial world, and the temptation is to conclude on a note of solid empiricism. Yet I shall resist this temptation in order to explore one last highly conjectural area that seems inescapable in any consideration of what the future may be like.

This is the classic problem of the economic "base" and the noneconomic "superstructure"—a problem that finds its starkest expression in Marx, but that can be traced back to the Scottish historical school. For a fact that must be admitted, in all our conjecturings about the shape of things to come, is that we reveal ourselves, wittingly or otherwise, to be economic determinists—indeed, even technological determinists. To put it differently, all speculation about postindustrialism assumes that the causal line of inference runs *from* the economic changes *to* the political and social changes, and although feedbacks may be discussed (such as the drive toward plannification), the *primum mobile* of "prediction" is the economic dynamic of social evolution.

This primacy of economic dynamics has nothing to do with ideology. It arises because we can discern "law-like" motions within the economic sphere that have no counterparts in the political and social realms. However indistinct and blurred, these motions can nonetheless be described, and moreover, within broad limits their interactions can be deduced. One of these law-like motions is the drive for profits characteristic of a capitalist system. Although this drive does not produce the determinate "equilibrium" solutions of neo-classical economics,[26] it nonetheless permits us to anticipate with a fair degree of certainty such types of behavior as the search for cost-reducing technology, the concentration of business enterprise (whether for reasons of efficiency or profitable financial manipulation), the probable advent of economies of scale in industries that have not yet been "invaded" by technology, the crucial role to be played by autonomous public and private expenditures magnified by a "multiplier" of reasonably known dimensions, and still other regularities.

I hasten to stress the extreme tenuousness of our knowledge in all these fields. Short-run economic prediction, based on presumptively "known" behavioral functions and technical constraints, has been shown to be egregiously faulty. But this constraint does not apply with quite the same force to the longer run, when the persistent trends of economic life assert themselves over their short-term vagaries.[27] Hence to whatever extent we dare to predict the contours of postindustrial society, it is perforce on the basis of these economic projections. For what "law-like" statements can we apply to the organization of political affairs, to social organization, to changes in cultural lifestyle, and the like? Apart from a few descriptive generalizations —Michels' "iron law" of oligarchy, Weber's description of bureaucratic organization, Freud's or Erikson's outline of the topography of the psyche and its developmental stages—what do the other social sciences have to offer by way of predictive theory? The answer, I fear, is discouraging little. Thus, however inaccurate or inadequate the economic determinist view may be, it is foisted upon us as an initial mode of viewing the future for lack of any alternative "positive" approach.

This raises very grave problems for social scientists in our position. Not only are the "laws of motion" of economics extremely imprecise, but the linkages between any given economic structure and its interlocked political and social accoutrements are even more difficult to describe with any degree of assurance. I must confess to a suspicion that if postindustrial society follows the general economic trajectory I have described, it will be accompanied by a more authoritarian political structure, by more anomic groups in the undereducated, by increasing restlessness and boredom among the educated "middle classes" still subject to the stimuli of a competitive, acquisitive culture. But this is only conjecture; perhaps one can draw equally or more convincing scenarios of greater stability, communal morale, individual fulfillment.

In this situation of extreme indeterminacy a key may be provided by what Adolph Lowe has identified as the mood of the times—certainly of the postindustrial age. He calls this "the end of social fatalism."[28] By this he means the end of an age in which not only the events of nature, but the events of society, are taken as "givens" to be mutely accepted by the uncomplaining masses, or explained away in terms of a theological or a political religion.

If this identification of a profound change in mood is true—and I believe that it is—perhaps our view of the future

43

as something to be "predicted" is fundamentally at variance with the realities of the age. In an era that has rejected social fatalism, the future will no longer "arrive," but it will be *made*, however crudely, cruelly, or well by the harnessing of political wills and their focusing on deliberately chosen goals. It may therefore be quite mistaken to search, within economics or in its sister disciplines, for "positive" perspectives on a future which will not come into being by the workings of "law-like" mechanisms (although it may be influenced by their residual influence), but by the political selection of social goals whose means of attainment then becomes the subject for social scientific investigation.[29]

This leaves open, of course, the choice of goals. About this all-important question the social scientist has nothing to say, either as counselor or as expert "prognosticator." Perforce he relinquishes his place to the moral philosopher—his historical godfather—whose task it is to raise the consciousness of men to the alternatives open to them. The goals once chosen, the social scientist again comes into his own in the more modest, but nonetheless important, role of social "engineer." If there is one ultimate definition for postindustrial society, then, I would suggest it is that stage of socio-economic organization in which men gradually escape from the thralldom of blind mechanisms to enter the perilous, but potentially liberating, terrain in which human beings finally assert themselves, for better or worse, as the masters of their fate.

Notes

1. This statement implies a certain economic determinism. I will deal specifically with this issue at the end of this essay.

2. A long literature—too long for a note—now deals with postindustrial society. The most sophisticated version of the concept is to be found in Daniel Bell's work: see

especially the symposium, including his essay, in *Survey,* Winter, 1971; "The Post-Industrial Society: The Evolution of an Idea," *Survey,* Spring, 1971; and *The Coming of Post-Industrial Society* (1973). Reference should also be made to Zbigniew Brzezinski's *Between Two Ages: America's Role in the Technetronic Era* (1970). A more simplistic and quantitative exploration of the term is to be found in Herman Kahn's and Anthony Wiener's *The Year 2000* (1967). Numerous books have popularized the idea, of which the currently most widely quoted is Alvin Toffler's *Future Shock* (1971).

3. In England in 1811 less than a third of the work force was employed in agriculture, and over a third was in services throughout the first half of the nineteenth century. (B. R. Mitchell, *Abstract of British Historical Statistics* (1962), p. 60; S. Kuznets, *Modern Economic Growth* (1966), p. 106.

4. Transportation and utilities, because they produce nontangible commodities, are often grouped within the tertiary sector; and mining in the primary sector. I group them here in the "industrial" sector because they are integrally connected with industrial processes.

5. The reader should be warned that these statistics must be interpreted with care. For example, some of the decline in employment in the agricultural sector represents a shift of agriculture-related employment into the industrial and service sectors—e.g., the rise of farm machinery manufacture, of chemical fertilizers, and of a government service sector and a private trade sector occupied with agricultural problems and products. Thus the employment *functionally* related to agriculture is larger, perhaps by a considerable degree, than that "formally" related to it. See S. Lebergott, *Manpower in Economic Growth* (1964), p. 111. Nevertheless, the basic shift is unambiguously out of rural pursuits, "through" industry, and into service tasks.

6. The literature is again too large to be reviewed. Key statements are those of M. Abramovitz, *Resource and Out-*

45

put *Trends in the United States since 1870,* National Bureau of Economic Research (1956); Robert Solow, "Technical Change and the Aggregate Production Function," *Review of Economics and Statistics,* (August 1957); and Edward Denison, *Sources of Economic Growth in the United States,* Commission for Economic Development, (1962).

7. Denison, *Sources of Economic Growth.*

8. Ferenc Janossy, *The End of the Economic Miracle* (1971), has a dramatic imaginative illustration of the respective importance of knowledge versus "labor power" or "capital." He asks us to imagine the instantaneous transfer of the populations of two nations, one developed and one underdeveloped—say England and Pakistan (before its civil war). Is there any doubt, he asks, that the growth curve of "Pakistan" would rapidly turn upward; while that of "England" would soon turn sharply down?

9. John M. Blair, *Economic Concentration* (1972), p. 15, citing estimate by David Novick of the Rand Corporation.

10. *The Sources of Invention* (1958, rev. ed., 1969). See also Blair, *Economic Concentration,* pp. 215-27.

11. See among others, Bell, *Coming of Post-Industrial Society,* Brzezinski, *Between Two Ages,* J. K. Galbraith, *The New Industrial State,* (1967) and my own *The Limits of American Capitalism,* (1966).

12. Perhaps it is to be noted in passing that the same ambivalence also attaches to this new figure who is viewed, as was the older entrepreneur, both as a heroic personage capable of building a great society and as a demonic force capable of destroying it.

13. Blair, *Economic Concentration,* ch. 4.

14. Averitt, *The Dual Economy,* 1968.

15. Blair, *Economic Concentration,* 152 and passim

16. Howard Sherman, *Radical Political Economy* (1972), pp. 110, 113-14.

17. For a few studies of these linkages see: AEA *Proceedings,* 1972, pp. 279-318, esp. articles by Kaufman and Melman; Robert Engler, *The Politics of Oil* (1961); G. Kolko, *The Triumph of Conservatism,* (1963); H. Kariel, *The Decline of American Pluralism* (1961).

18. See A. Schonfield, *Modern Capitalism,* (1965).

19. See G. Kolko, *Wealth and Power in America* (1962). Also, Ackerman, Birnbaum, Wetzler and Zimbalist, "The Extent of Income Inequality in the United States" in *The Capitalist System,* ed. R. Edwards, M. Reich, T. Weisskopf (1972).

20. Robert Lampman, *The Share of Top Wealth Holders in National Wealth,* National Bureau of Economic Reseach (1962), p. 24.

21. Let me simply remind the reader that this sector includes the most highly bureaucratized elements of American life—the federal government—and the least bureaucratized—the individual proprietor or professional in the service trades or profession; very highly skilled tasks (surgeons) and very low-skilled (filing clerks); the very highly paid (entertainers) and the very poorly paid (servants).

22. Joan Robinson has suggested (*Economic Heresies,* p. 93) that control over the price level ultimately depends on the acquiesence of the population in a "traditional" set of hierarchical gradations, so that the determination of a few key wage bargains in fact settles the aggregate wage bill. The increasing "white collar" nature of work and the greater educational exposure of the majority may lessen this means of internalized control, unleashing a "free-for-all" race which no mechanism other than outright controls will be able to restrain.

23. A brief technical note seems necessary here. Technology releases the manpower, but its migration into another sector thereafter depends on the demand for commodities originating in the various sectors. Had the demand for ag-

ricultural output been extremely elastic, the release of labor through mechanization would have resulted only in a much vaster increase in total farm output than we have in fact experienced. The same applies to manufacturing. It is not only technology, but the inelasticity of demand for "food" (Engel's Law) and the approximately unitary elasticity for manufactured goods that have resulted in the precipitous fall in rural employment and the secular steadiness of manufacturing employment.

24. See J. Schmookler, *Invention and Economic Growth,* (1966) for evidence of the role of demand in directing the course of technological discovery and application.

25. See Robert Heilbroner, "Growth and Survival," *Foreign Affairs* (October 1972) and, with J. Allentuck, "Ecological Balance and the Stationary State," *Journal of Land Economics,* (October 1972.)

26. On this point, see especially the discussion by A. Lowe, *On Economic Knowledge,* 1965, 1966.

27. See R. Heilbroner, "On the Limits of Economic Prediction, *Between Capitalism and Socialism.*

28. Adolph Lowe, "Is Present Day Higher Education 'Relevant'?" *Social Research,* Fall, 1971.

29. See again the work of Lowe, *On Economic Knowledge* and "Is Present Day Higher Education 'Relevant'?", and my essay "On the Possibility of a Political Economics," *Journal of Economic Issues,* December 1970.

Chapter Three

The Transition
to a Welfare
Economy in Japan

Hirofumi Uzawa

Since the end of World War II, Japan has experienced an impressive, rapid rate of economic growth, enabling it not only to recover from the vast ruins left after the war, but also to become one of the most industrialized and wealthiest countries in the world. At the same time this growth has been characterized by two trends which cannot—indeed, should not—continue in the future as in the immediate past.

The first is the nature of the social and economic reform introduced during the period when Japan was occupied by the Allied powers. The core of the reform was the strengthening of the private enterprise, competitive market economic system where each individual might pursue his own interest without explicit regard to the interest of the society, and where the possible conflict between individuals was left for resolution by the forces of the market. Naturally, it would be a gross overstatement to say that such arrangements did not exist in prewar Japan. They were, however, by no means as important as they have become in the postwar period when the market system has come to be the dominant element in shaping the Japanese economy and the society at large. This reform created a social milieu in which human resources could be fully developed and effectively utilized, in contrast to the prewar situation where human beings were subject to rigid regimentation and their abilities were in a sense frozen and distorted.

On the other hand, the introduction of such a system into Japanese society by abrupt grafting rather than gradual evolution had certain undesirable effects. One of the most conspicuous has been the relative failure of either the individuals concerned or the society at large to give due attention to the social costs of unrestrained entrepreneurial activity, with the result that real individual living levels have become more unequal.

This is not to deny that the distribution of nominal income in Japan has had a tendency to be equalized over the past twenty years. Rather, it is to recognize that there may be a significant difference between the *real* living standard as a measure of the values available to an individual, which include, for example, opportunities for education, cultural participation, or enjoyment of health, and the *nominal* income as measured by the size of his pay envelope. And it is to point out that inequities in the real living standards of the Japanese people have not been reduced so much as the rate of economic growth would indicate. This has been primarily due to the fact that during the process of economic growth, the natural environment has been depleted and the social infrastructure has been neglected, with the cost falling heavily on the poor, who have not had much freedom in choosing an occupation and a place to live.

The extent to which this has happened may be illustrated by the recent incidence of poisoning due to industrial residuals. This problem of environmental pollution has become a concern of many industrialized countries in recent years, but Japan is unique in having a large number of serious victims caused by such residuals. In the Minamata incident, for example, more than one hundred people have had their nervous systems permanently damaged by the mercury poisoning resulting from the residuals emitted from a factory of one of southern Japan's largest chemical companies. It is now estimated that those affected may eventually number several thousand in a region of less than half a million population. The victims, of course, are mostly poor inhabitants who have no choice but to continue living in this contaminated region. Minamata is a symbol of the poverty which still prevails in a country that takes pride in being the third largest industrial power in the world, and of the agony which industrial contamination has inflicted on the poor.

The adverse effect of unrestrained entrepreneurial activity has been compounded by a second aspect of Japan's postwar economy: the single-minded emphasis of successive governments on economic growth, seen as the maximization of such aggregate economic indices as the gross national product (GNP) or the real national income, which takes into account only those goods and services that may be transacted in the market. Factors which are not involved in the market mechanism, such as the depreciation of the environment or the social costs borne by the poor have been largely ignored in the planning and execution of economic policy. Instead, the Japanese government has concentrated almost exclusively on increasing the nation's industrialization and export activities as fast as possible, occasionally even at the expense of the economic welfare of the people and the international stability of the world. As a result, Japan indeed has attained an extremely high rate of growth in GNP and other aggregate measures. This was manifest particularly in the sixties when a very vigorous industrialization program was carried out.

However, the Minamata incident and others involving environmental pollution have so attracted the attention of the public in the last few years that attitudes concerning industrialization and economic growth are now almost completely changed. Many rural regions which were previously eager to have industrial complexes built in their own regions have begun to question the wisdom of such a policy. Because of the popular resentment toward the social cost associated with industrial activities, it has indeed become more and more difficult for industrial firms to find locations to build their factories. At the same time, many urban regions have begun to tighten the regulatory measures concerning pollution and other environmental disruption, and existing factories have been forced more and more to take necessary measures to reduce the levels of industrial residuals. One can anticipate a fairly significant increase in investment in pollution abatement, rising from approximately 1 percent of GNP at the end of the sixties to about 2 percent in 1974.

A very similar phenomenon has been taking place concerning the use of automobiles and the construction of highways. In Japan, there are roughly 20 million automobiles, that is, one automobile for every five persons. This per capita figure may not be regarded as excessive compared with other advanced countries, but the number of automobiles in Japan per acre of inhabitable land is extremely high, about ten times that in the United States. Automobile accidents in Japan are now numbering about 20,000 deaths and 1,000,000 injuries a year. These figures too may not be regarded as excessive compared with other advanced countries. But again, if one looks at the substantive aspect, one can see that the Japanese situation is rather extraordinary. Of the 20,000 deaths due to automobile accidents, more than 50 percent are those of pedestrians and bicycle riders, compared with the American figure of about 15 percent. This is primarily due to the fact that in major Japanese cities very few roads have separate pedestrian walks.

Even in the city of Tokyo, the majority of streets are less than twenty feet wide. It is physically impossible to construct separate walks for pedestrians and the manner in which automobiles are driven indicates that those who walk on the street are not accorded very high esteem. The maze of highways which has been constructed right through the center of Tokyo reflects the general lack of concern for the environment.

During this period of rapid economic growth, the automobile industry was felt to be a pivotal one for promoting economic growth. It was also a symbol of individual freedom. But the heavy death tolls due to automobile accidents, together with the serious environmental destruction resulting from both highway construction and automobile driving, have begun to affect the thinking of the general public. Many people in Japan have become concerned for the preservation of their environment and resistant to the indiscriminate use of automobiles and construction of highways. While the economic and political weight of the automobile and construction industries impedes this change in national values, the fact that change is taking place may be seen in the significant increase in the number of citizens' movements to preserve the environment. More than that, one may reasonably expect this shift in values to accelerate over the next decade and begin to effect changes in Japan's environment. It may be helpful to conceptualize such changes in terms broadly applicable, not just to Japan but to the industrialized world in general.

The market-oriented economy, which we have noted as fundamental to the institutional arrangements of postwar Japanese society, has two distinctive features. The first is related to the process of allocating scarce resources. Such a system presupposes that the limited resources in production and consumption are privately owned and are disposed of in such a manner that private benefits, either in the form of profits or utilities, are maximized. Market institutions are those which resolve possible conflicts between various members of that society without resorting to regulatory measures.

The second feature of a market economy is related to distribution. In such a system each individual is entitled to receive rewards for the scarce resources he owns according to the evaluation of the market, and nothing more or less. Thus, if an individual's own resources are relatively scarce and highly appreciated in the market, his income will be larger; otherwise, he has to be satisfied with whatever income he gets. This feature helps the market mechanism to attain an efficient allocation of resources. But it has an unfortunate effect on the distribution of real income from the welfare point of view. In particular, such a rewarding arrangement has a tendency to increase the degree of income inequality, particularly among the generations. This tendency has been long recognized as inherent in the market economy and various measures such as progressive income taxes and inheritance taxes, have been adopted by most contemporary societies in an attempt to offset it. The effect of such arrangements has been not so much to help the individual to stay above the poverty line as to rescue those who may have dropped below it.

It is one of the most basic propostions in economic theory that such a market mechanism brings about an efficient allocation of scarce resources. This proposition crucially depends upon the institutional arrangements whereby all the resources are privately owned. In most advanced democratic societies, however, either for technological reasons or for reasons of social justice, a very significant portion of scarce resources are not privately appropriated or owned. Instead, they are owned by the society; the responsibility for such resources—their preservation, use, construction or management—is delegated to the government, and they generally are used by the members of the society, either free of charge or for a nominal price. Sometimes referred to as social overhead capital, they have not been the subject of thorough economic analysis. Yet it is clear that they have always played a very important role in the processes of resource allocation and Income distribution in all contemporary market economies. It is also clear that the economic issues of the future are going to revolve more and more around the use of these resources.

We may begin to think about these matters by recognizing social overhead capital as including three categories of resources: natural, social, and institutional. Natural capital is that overhead capital which is in general difficult to reproduce such as air, water, forest and so forth. Social capital refers to such things as roads, ports, bridges, sewage systems, educational and medical facilities, which may be reproduced and maintained by the state to provide basic services to the members of the society. The third category consists of institutions such as judicial systems, market systems, and monetary institutions, which provide the members of the society with institutional services.

This social overhead capital constitutes what may be called the environment in a very wide sense of the word. Its role increases as the process of economic growth takes place and the level of living increases. Of course, the classification of scarce resources between private and social overhead capital is not absolute; it depends upon the social, historical, and political conditions prevailing in any given society.

In a purely decentralized, private-enterprise economy, the services derived from such overhead capital are generally provided free of charge or at a minimal price. On the other hand, the supply of such social overhead resources, in particular the natural capital, are limited compared with the magnitude of private capital so that the resulting allocation of scarce resources is neither efficient nor optimum. Furthermore, the degree of inefficiency in the allocation of scarce resources through the competitive market process is increased as the process of capital accumulation is accelerated, particularly with respect to the natural environment. Natural capital is difficult or impossible to reproduce and it becomes more and more scarce in relation to private means of production. Hence, the imputed value of the natural environment to the society becomes very great, particularly in Japan where the level of industrial activity per acre of land is extremely high compared with other countries. Still, there is no inherent mechanism which takes account of the scarcity of such natural environment in a market economy. The resulting environmental pollution becomes insidious.

In a sense, this phenomenon of environmental pollution

55

may be regarded as an outcome of the mismanagement of social overhead capital; but in a purely market economy there is very little incentive to regularize the use of such social overhead capital. Thus, in the market economy of Japan the intrinsic tendency toward inequal income distribution has been aggravated by an inequitable allocation of social costs during the process of economic growth in the last decade. The resulting problems now force us to reexamine the basic institutional arrangements underlying the market economy, to gradually adopt social and economic policies which give priority to the economic welfare of the members of the society, and to try to restore social stability in the allocative mechanism.

The institutional framework adapted to the postindustrial society, particularly in Japan, would therefore seem to be that of the welfare state. By this I mean a state in which the social institutional arrangements are concerned primarily with the equity of income distribution as well as the efficiency of resource allocation. The fundamental purpose of social and economic institutions in such a society would be to guarantee that every citizen is accorded a decent standard of living in both economic and physical aspects, regardless of his income and wealth. Although the recognition of a citizen's basic right to a decent and healthy life is a recent phenomenon in Japan—indeed, it was only during the occupation that it was inspired by the incorporation of socal rights in the new constitution—this expanded notion of the basic rights of the citizen constitutes the most fundamental aspect of contemporary society.

It is difficult to define precisely these basic rights, for their meaning has grown over time. Until the middle of the nineteeth century, as typically explained by Payne or Mill, these rights were conceived of as elements of civil liberty; they consisted largely of freedom of thought, religion, choice of profession, and residence. The market economy was regarded as the best institution for implementing such a concept and the neoclassical economics of Jevons, Menger, and others in the 1870s was regarded as the best theoretical explanation of this institution.

But toward the end of the nineteenth century and during the first half of the twentieth century, the allocative mechanism of the market economy began to create rather insidious economic and social disturbances, resulting mostly from the chronic resurgence of depression and unemployment. At the same time, the content of the basic rights of the citizen were significantly expanded to include the concept of full employment and minimum subsistence. That is, every citizen was now felt to be entitled to enjoy not only basic civil rights, but also the right to be gainfully employed and to live at least at a subsistence level; and the government was held responsible to adopt such economic measures as might be required to secure for the citizen these new rights. The economic theory of Keynes' *General Theory* may be regarded as an attempt to explain how to implement such policy objectives. During World War II, another significant contribution to the new concept was made by the 1942 Report of the Beveridge Committee. To the rights of civil liberty and employment was added the right to a decent living standard, meaning something higher than elemental subsistence. How to construct the institutional framework for implementing such an enlarged concept of the basic rights of the citizen has now become one of the most crucial problems in the design of a welfare state. The welfare state of the future must see to it that every member of society is provided the services which are indispensable to his basic rights and must maintain the institutional, physical, and human resources which are needed to provide such services.

The exact nature of the services a government will be called on to provide must be determined by the society for itself and will depend substantially on the historical and social conditions of that society. But it may be proposed as a general economic guideline that the state should provide those services which are indispensable to the basic rights of the citizen. This includes services having a low elasticity of demand with respect to price, which would result in an inequitable distribution if supplied through a market mechanism.

Major components of such services would be medical care, basic education, and basic transportation, together with the services of police forces, fire brigades, and so forth. These functions will occupy an important part of the services to be publicly provided in a welfare state. The fact that they are provided to the members of the society in fact significantly lowers the probability that the average person will drop out of the society from an economic point of view.

One rather difficult problem confronting the design of a welfare state is that certain scarce resources such as the natural environment are difficult or impossible to increase. The imputed value to the society therefore is very high. If the services from such capital are provided free of charge, the phenomenon of pollution inevitably occurs. It is necessary, therefore, for the state to regulate the use of services from such social resources, requiring the members of society to pay a price which is equal to the marginal social cost associated with the use of such services.

The larger the stock of social capital, the less scarce it will be and, therefore, the lower will be the price. However, at the same time, the larger the stock of social capital, the greater will be the cost of maintenance or expansion of such capital, and therefore the larger will be the deficits incurred by the government for the provision of such services. An increase in the stock of social overhead capital will imply an increase in overall taxes so that in determining the level of social overhead capital to be provided, one has to take into account the opportunity cost associated with the construction and the maintenance of such capital.

Another pressing problem is the construction of new statistical measures which, unlike GNP, can reflect these new welfare concerns, so that institutions can be perfected for stabilizing the distributional aspects of such institutions.

In the sixties the Japanese government adopted such

policy measures as credit expansion and export subsidies, and allocated a fairly significant portion of public investment to the construction of an industrial infrastructure. According to one estimate, about 80 percent of public investment was spent on the construction and maintenance of the industrial infrastructure, leaving only a very small portion to be spent on the maintenance of social overhead capital directly concerned with the health and living standards of the people. Such a pattern of public investment may be justified only if the policy objectives do not include significantly the non-market aspects of economic performance.

In a welfare state, the primary objective of the government is to ensure the harmonious development of economic welfare, which takes into account not only the level of personal income, but also the extent of the services available from social overhead capital. This implies an increase in total public expenditures and a significant shift toward public expenditures for the maintenance of social capital directly involved with living standards and the preservation of the natural environment. Investment in the industrial infrastructure will have to be slowed down. This will result in an overall increase in manufacturing costs and in the short run will accelerate the rise of prices generally. In the long run, however, it would be conducive to a more stable pattern of price increase.

There would be another adverse short-run effect of the change in public financial policy in as much as it would entail a significant shift in the management of the natural environment. The use of services and destruction of natural capital would be more strictly regulated, either in the form of effluent charges, or in the form of ambient standards more directly concerned with the preservation of the environment. Such regulatory measures would have adverse effects upon the process of economic growth and would alter the composition of the GNP. But again, such adverse effects can be expected to be of a short-run nature, and when the economy is fully adjusted to the new regulatory measures, it would become possible to maintain a stable and relatively high rate of growth, even in terms of the conventional national income account. This phenomenon is due primarily to the fact that natural and social environments constitute a vital factor in the processes of production and consumption, and only by taking measures that reflect their scarcity in using them is it possible to achieve a long-run stable path of economic growth.

Part III
The Polity

Chapter Four

Japanese Politics in Flux

Joji Watanuki

The changes in Japan's economy over the past fifteen years have been vast. For example, the percentage of the population engaged in agriculture dropped from 40 percent in 1955 to 20 percent in 1970, and the GNP increased from $25 billion to roughly $200 billion in the same period (see Table 4-1); but the impact of these changes on Japan's society and politics is still to be seen.

Generally speaking, the greatest impact has been felt on the style of consumption. Ownership of television sets, washing machines, and refrigerators has increased dramatically. By 1965 over 90 percent of all Japanese households owned black and white television sets. By 1970 most also owned washing machines; and refrigerators lagged only slightly behind. Then, just as the distribution of these three products was reaching a near saturation point, sales promoters and journalists began to herald a new wave of consumer demands, this time for the "three c's": a color television, an air conditioner, and a car. Taste in food also has changed: the Japanese today eat less rice and more meat, eggs, and fruits.

Such changes in consumption style have occurred not only in cities, but also in rural areas. Although the rural population has declined in size, it has not declined in income. In fact, rural income has kept pace with and in some cases

Table 4-1
Some Indicators of Change in Japanese Economy and Society, 1955-1980

	1955	1960	1970	1980 est.
GNP (billion US $)[a]	24.6	45.5	203.3	1000.0 (1985)
Per capita income (US $)[b]	222	382	1536	3874
Labor force[c]				
primary industry (%)	41.0	32.6	19.3	10.3
secondary industry	23.5	29.2	33.9	35.3
tertiary industry	35.5	38.2	46.7	54.3
Employment status:[d]				
self-employed (%)	23.9	22.0	19.3	
family worker	30.3	24.0	16.2	
employed	45.8	54.0	64.5	
Urbanization (%)[e]		43.7	53.5	
Spread of higher education (%)[f]	8.8	10.2	18.9	31.9
Ratio of nuclear family (%)[g]	62.0	63.4	68.1	

[a] 1955-1970, from Keizai Kikakuchō, *Kokumin shotoku tōkei nenkan* [Statistical yearbook of national income], 1972, converted into U.S. $ by the then prevailing rate of 1 U.S. $ = 360 Yen. Figures for 1985 are from Prime Minister Kakuei Tanaka, *Ninon rettō kaizōron* [Proposals to remodel the Japanese Islands] (Tokyo: Nikkan Kogyo Shinbunsha, 1972), p. 65.

[b] 1955, 1960 from *UN Statistical Yearbook*. 1970 from *UN Monthly Report of Statistics*. 1980 from an estimate made by *Kokumin Keizai Kenkyu Kyokai*, 1972.

[c] 1955, 1960, 1970 from Census. 1980 from an estimate by *Nihon Keizai Kenkyu Senta*.

[d] Same as note c.

[e] Census. Percentage of the population living in densely populated districts (more than 4,000 persons per square kilometer).

[f] 1955, 1960, 1970 from Nonbusho, *Nihon no kyōiku tōkei-Meiji-Shōwa* [Japanese educational statistics from Meiji to Showa], 1971. Estimate for 1980 is taken from Monbusho, *Monbu Koho*, [Education report] July 13, 1971.

[g] Census. Ratio of number of nuclear type households to total number of households.

surpassed that of urban dwellers. This has been due in part to protective measures taken by the government, which have guaranteed the price of rice, provided subsidies for improving agricultural facilities, and maintained a high tariff on agricultural products from abroad. It is explained also by the increased demand for seasonal labor, especially by the construction industry, which provides opportunities for farmers to earn a cash income during off seasons. Thus the homogenization of consumption styles has become conspicuous throughout Japan.

This new style has been colored particularly by the rise in the economic status of youth. Since long before World War II Japanese employment had been characterized by a wage and promotion system based on seniority and a preference for life-long employment.[1] These characteristics survived the reforms of the postwar period, in some ways becoming more deeply ingrained than before. In the late sixties, however, a labor shortage developed. Young people, whose average wage was far lower than that of their seniors, were quick to press for higher wages. As a result, wages for young workers have begun to rise more rapidly than those for senior workers. In addition, opportunities for part-time jobs for university students have increased. Thus the purchasing power of young people has jumped and a vast youth market for consumer goods has been formed. Shrewd businessmen have taken advantage of this change, catering to a new youth taste throughout the country. The "three c's" are being accompanied by miniskirts, leather boots, blue jeans, maxicoats, bowling alleys, midnight snackbars, and weekend ski resorts.

The recent experience of Japan, like that of Europe and the United States, would seem to demonstrate that where there is a significant increase in personal income, a freewheeling private enterprise system, and no strong state, religious or other inhibitions on taste, the outward style of a people's life can be changed in a short period of time indeed. But what of the inner life, the world of the mind where values reign? Have the great changes in Japan's economy exerted a similarly strong impact on this realm as well? Does a young Japanese man in his colorful shirt and wide tie or a young Japanese woman in her miniskirt and leather boots think at all like an American or West European youth with similar consumer tastes? Or underneath these new styles does the young Japanese still share the values of the older generation?

One would expect of course that the value system and the frame of reference of a people would change to some extent in a situation like that of postwar Japan where no official efforts at indoctrination have been made and no strong religious inhibitions have been operative; but the experience of Japan is that even under such conditions, the values of a people change rather slowly and they change differentially with the generations. There has been a time lag between the diffusion of the new consumption style in Japan and the spread of new values congruent with this style. A gap also has opened between the generations, the young being readier than the old to accept both the new style and the new values associated with it.

Since 1953 the Institute of Statistical Mathematics in Tokyo has conducted a nationwide survey of Japanese national character every five years, using many of the same questions. A comparison of the answers obtained in successive surveys shows that over this period, some values have changed and some have not. Apparently there has been a slow but steady decline of such traditional values, for example, as the importance of family continuity, devotion to the Shinto cult, and respect for political leaders (see Table 4-2). On the other hand, as shown in Table 4-3, such an attitude as preference for a paternalistic supervisor, so different from American attitudes, appears to show no change over time or between the generations.

This attitude, however, seems to be exceptional. Most attitudes showing change also show a remarkable age differential, and the marginal change in the time series suggests that the new attitudes will continue to spread more and more as the present young generation grows older and new generations come on the scene. A typical example of this is the growing attitude that one should live one's life, "to suit one's own taste."[2] The percentage of people in their early twenties (20-24 years old) who express this attitude has steadily increased from 32 percent in 1953, to 38 percent in 1958, to 44 percent in 1963, to 52 percent in 1968. If we simply extrapo-

Table 4-2

Some Examples of Recent Changes in Japanese National Attitudes

Item	1st Survey (1953) (%)	4th Survey (1968 (%)
"If you have no children, do you think it necessary to adopt a child in order to continue the family line, even if there is no blood relationship? Or do you not think this is important?"		
Yes, would adopt	73	43
"There are all sorts of attitudes toward life. Of those listed here [card shown] which one would you say comes closest to your feeling?"		
Resist all evils in the world and live a pure and just life (Traditional)	29	17
Don't think about money or fame; just live a life that suits your own tastes (Nontraditional)	21	32
"Some Prime Ministers, when they take office, pay a visit to the Imperial Shrine at Ise. What do you think about this practice?"		
Should go	57	31
Can do as he pleases (Nontraditional)	23	33
Better not to go; or should not go (Nontraditional)	8	20
"Some people say that if we get good political leaders the best way to improve the country is for the people to leave everything to them, rather than for the people to discuss things among themselves. Do you agree with this or disagree?"		
Agree should leave up to leaders (Traditional)	43	30
"If a person were presented with a choice between attending a patron's death bed or attending a crucially important meeting of his firm, which should he do?"[a]		
Leave everything and go home (Traditional)	54	46
Go to the meeting (Nontraditional)	41	47

[a]A reduced version of the actual question asked.

Source: This table is a reduced version of the fourth nationwide survey conducted in the fall of 1968 by the *Tōkei Sūri Kenkyūjō Kokuminsei Chōsa Iinkai*, as reported in *Nihonjin no kokuminsei* [Japanese national character]2 (Tokyo: Shiseido, 1970): 535, 558-59.

late this trend into the future, by 1980 it may be expected that an overwhelming proportion of young people will share this conception; and if we dare to use this as an indicator of "post-industrial values,"[3] it would appear that postindustrial values may well predominate in Japanese society in the near future.

Additional data indicate that another attitudinal trend has begun to take shape in recent years, that connected with the environmental problem. Air and water pollution and other environmental destruction caused by the economic growth of the 1960s has come suddenly to be highlighted by the mass media. Movements against pollution and environmental destruction have erupted in various industrial zones where residents up to now had tolerated the sufferings caused by industrial pollution in the belief that pollution was a necessary by-product of industry and that the prosperity of the industrial enterprise was essential to that of the community and the individual. But postindustrial values are evident in the results of a survey conducted in 1972 in which health and life are preferred more than money and wealth, and nature more than economic development (see Table 4-4). However people are still very much concerned with their income, the same survey showing that a larger income is more desired than a shorter workweek and indeed that a shorter workweek is desired by most only if income is not affected. It is apparent, therefore, that "industrial values," emphasizing income and work, remain strong. Furthermore, such traditional values as the preference for a paternalistic supervisor are still cherished by many. Thus, among the Japanese people today, three value systems have come to coexist: traditional, industrial, and postindustrial.

The question we now turn to is, How are these value systems reflected in politics? First of all, let us look into the people's preferences for each of the political parties, and how this affects the total pattern of politics through elections and consequent distribution of the seats in the Diet.

We have seen that over the past decade there has been a shift in the value structure away from those attitudes imbued with tradition and even those fostered by the industrial soci-

Table 4-3
Some Examples of Japanese Attitudes Which Have Remained Virtually Unchanged

	1st survey (1953) (%)	4th survey (1968) (%)
"If you think a thing is right, do you think you should go ahead and do it even if it is contrary to usual custom, or do you think you are less apt to make a mistake if you follow custom?"		
Go ahead (Nontraditional)	41	42
Follow custom (Traditional)	35	34
"There are all sorts of attitudes toward life. Of those listed here [card shown], which would you say comes closest to your feeling?"		
Work hard and get rich	15	17
"Suppose you are working in a firm. There are two types of department chiefs. [chart shown] Which of these two would you prefer to work under?"[a]		
A man who always sticks to the work rules and never demands any unreasonable work, but on the other hand, never does anything for you personally in matters not connected with the work (Nonpaternalistic)	12	12
A man who sometimes demands extra work in spite of rules against it, but on the other hand, looks after you personally in matters not connected with the work. (Paternalistic)	85	84
"Which one of the following opinions do you agree with?"		
If individuals are made happy, then and only then will Japan as a whole improve (Nontraditional)	25	27
If Japan as a whole improves, then and only then can individuals be made happy (Traditional)	37	32
Improving Japan and making individuals happy are the same thing	31	36

[a]An interesting contrast to Americans' attitudes is presented by Whitehill and Takezawa, who conducted a comparative study of the attitudes of workers in the United States and Japan, using the same questionnaire. "To a question concerning the proper behavior of a superior, when a worker wishes to marry, 70 percent of the Japanese respondents felt the supervisor should 'offer personal advice to the worker if requested,' while 60 percent of the American respondents felt the superior should 'not be involved in such a personal matter.'" Arthur M. Whitehill, Jr. and Shin'ichi Takezawa, *The Other Worker: A Comparative Study of Industrial Relations in the United States and Japan* (Honolulu: East-West Center Press, 1968), p. 171.

Source: Same as Table 4-2, pp. 538, 554, 563.

Table 4-4
Preferences of the Japanese People

"Among the following, which do you think the most important to you?"	
Life and health	47.0%
Family	21.2%
Love and friendship	9.8%
Nation, society, and politics	6.4%
Work and trust	5.3%
Children	5.2%
Money and wealth	2.6%
"Which do you think more important?"	
Preservation of nature	59.7%
Development (e.g., construction of roads, housing sites and factories)	20.2%
"Which of the following would you prefer?"	
Increase of income	43.3%
Shortening of work hours	16.2%
Can't choose (implies welcoming of shortened working hours on the condition that level of income is guaranteed)	33.1%

Source: *Keizai Shingikai Kokuminsenkōdo Chōsa Iinkai,* Kokumin sen kōdo chōsa—daiichigi shūkei kekkahōkoku [Preliminary report on the preferences of the people], 1972. The survey was conducted in May, 1972 of a 14,120 sample of the Japanese population of over fifteen years of age.

ety of the recent past, and toward those more congruent with the postindustrial order now emerging. One might suppose therefore that this would be reflected in a similar shift in voter allegiance away from the more conservative and toward the more reformist parties. Such indeed was the expectation of most observers of the Japanese scene a decade ago. The emergence of postindustrial values was not then foreseen, but the cleavage of Japanese society between traditionalists and modernists was everywhere apparent. In this circumstance, Japanese politics seemed best understood as "cultural politics," that is, as a competition for power between tradition-oriented groups, who supported the Liberal Democratic party, (LDP), and the "modern" sectors of society, who supported the opposition parties.[4] From this perspective, since the modern sectors of society were gaining steadily at the expense of the traditional sectors, it seemed reasonable to expect within the foreseeable future that a fundamental political change would take place: the conservative party would be voted out and a new and powerful coalition of Socialist-led reformist forces would come to power.

The concept of "cultural politics" was not wholly wrong. In 1972 as in 1960, it was the tradition-oriented groups —farmers, fishermen, merchants, small manufacturers, the less highly educated and older people—who supported the conservative party most strongly (see Tables 4-5, 4-6, and 4-7.) In contrast, the modern sectors of the population —white-collar workers, manual workers, the more highly educated and the young (when they vote)—still preferred the opposition parties. This evidence is supported by the results of a survey conducted in 1972 which show that the correlation between holders of traditional values and supporters of the LDP is still fairly high.[5]

Moreover, as the proportion of the tradition-oriented groups in society declined, so did the strength of the conservative party. By 1972, for example, popular support for the LDP had dropped from 63.2 percent in 1955 to 46.9 percent (see Table 4-8). This drop reflected the decline in the proportion of farmers among the Japanese working force from 40 percent to 20 percent over the same period. Contrary to expectations, however, the LDP drop did not reflect it exactly. Conservative strength has held up better than expected and after a decade of fundamental changes in the socioeconomic structure of the country, the Liberal Democrats remain in power.

There would seem to be three reasons for this turn of events. As indicated by the increase in "Don't Know" responses between 1960 and 1969 (see Tables 4-5, 4-6, and 4-7), the number of persons who are reluctant to name the party whose candidate they have supported has grown. Another development may be related to this: if one breaks down the data on the socioeconomic bases of party support according to the size of community, one discovers that the more highly

Table 4-5
Party Voting by Occupational Groups, 1960 and 1972

November 1960[a] (in Percentages)

	LDP	JSP	DSP	Miscellaneous	Nonpartisan Candidates	"Don't Know"	Nonvoter
Farmers and fishermen	70.1	17.5	3.6	0.3	0.3	1.4	6.8
Merchants and small manufacturers	64.8	19.6	4.0	0.6	1.2	—	9.7
White-collar workers	31.8	44.0	4.9	1.5	0.4	0.4	17.0
Manual workers	31.0	43.2	1.1	2.7	2.1	5.2	14.7
Housewives	51.2	25.2	5.4	0.3	0.6	3.2	14.0

December 1972[b]

	LDP	JSP	DSP	JCP	Komei	Non-partisan	"Don't Know"	Non-voter
Farmers and fishermen	68.6	7.6	—	1.3	1.3	1.9	16.1	3.2
Merchants and small manufacturers	53.6	10.7	1.5	6.4	2.8	0.7	15.0	9.3
White-collar workers	22.1	27.8	5.7	10.6	1.8	1.8	18.3	12.0
Manual workers	22.1	28.5	4.4	8.8	3.6	0.8	16.4	15.3
Housewives	31.0	21.5	3.4	5.3	4.5	1.4	18.9	13.9

[a]Joji Watanuki, "Patterns of Politics in Present-Day Japan," in Lipset and Rokkan, eds., *Party Systems and Voter Alignments*, p. 448, using data gathered by a nationwide sample survey conducted by Shinbun Yoron Chōsa Renmei [Public opinion survey league for the press] just after the election. At that time, the voters for JCP among the survey respondents were so few that they were put into "miscellaneous."

[b]Nationwide survey by Kōmei Senkyo Renmei, the report of which is to be published as *Dai 33-kai shugiingiin sōsenkyo no jittai* [A survey of the 33rd general election], 1973.

Table 4-6
Party Voting by a Comparison of Educational Level, 1960 and 1972 (in Percentages)

November 1960[a]	LDP	JSP	DSP	Miscel-laneous	Non-partisan Candidates	Don't Know	Non-voter
Low	57.0	22.2	4.0	0.6	0.4	1.9	13.9
Medium	46.2	34.8	5.0	0.7	0.9	0.7	11.6
High	39.2	35.0	7.7	—	2.1	—	16.1

December 1972[b]	LDP	JSP	DSP	JCP	Komei	Non-partisan	Don't Know	Non-voter
Low	41.6	16.5	3.3	4.4	4.4	1.2	17.4	11.2
Medium	32.7	21.0	2.9	7.8	2.2	1.5	18.0	14.0
High	31.7	17.5	5.3	8.0	1.5	1.2	19.5	15.3

[a]Watanuki, "Patterns of Politics," p. 449.
[b]Kōmei Senkyo Renmei.

73

Table 4-7
Party Voting by a Comparison of Age Groups, 1960 and 1972 (in Percentages)

November 1960[a]	LDP	JSP	DSP	Non-Miscellaneous	Non-partisan Candidates	Don't Know	Non-voter
20-29	37.6	37.1	5.1	1.2	0.3	0.5	18.1
30-39	50.1	32.2	4.9	0.4	0.3	0.3	11.3
40-49	59.4	23.0	5.1	0.2	1.0	2.0	9.4
50 over	62.8	15.0	3.7	0.5	0.9	2.6	14.5

December 1972[b]	LDP	JSP	DSP	JCP	Komei	Non-partisan	Don't Know	Non-voter
20-29	21.9	21.9	3.9	9.5	3.1	1.5	14.7	23.6
30-39	28.4	21.1	2.8	8.8	3.4	2.3	16.9	13.3
40-49	41.5	19.2	3.4	5.6	3.6	0.7	18.0	7.9
50-59	48.6	16.2	3.4	2.8	2.3	1.0	18.8	6.9
60 over	51.0	11.2	3.4	2.1	2.9	0.8	17.9	10.7

[a] Watanuki, "Patterns of Politics," p. 449.
[b] Kōmei Senkyo Renmei.

Table 4-8
Results of Elections to the House of Representatives by Party in 1955, 1958, 1969, and 1972[a]

February 1955	*Democrat*	*Liberal*	*Left Socialist*	*Right Socialist*	*Worker-Farmer*	*JCP*[b]	*Others*	*Total*
Vote (%)	36.6	26.6	15.3	13.9	1.0	2.0	4.6	100%
Seats	185	112	89	67	4	2	8	467
October 1958	*LDP*[c]	*JSP*[d]		*JCP*	*Others*	*Total*		
Vote (%)	57.8	32.9		2.6	6.7	100%		
Seats	287	166		1	13	467		
December 1969	*LDP*	*JSP*	*DSP*[e]	*Komei Party*[f]		*JCP*	*Others*	*Total*
Vote (%)	47.6	21.4	7.7	10.9		6.8	5.5	100%
Seats	288	90	31	47		14	16	486%
December 1972	*LDP*	*JSP*	*DSP*[e]	*Komei Party*[f]		*JCP*	*Others*	*Total*
Vote	46.9	21.9	7.0	8.4		10.5	5.3	100%
Seats	271	118	19	29		38	16	491

[a] Jichishō Senkyobu, *Shūgiin sōsenkyo kekka shirabe* [Report of the result of general election], published after each general election.

[b] Japan Communist Party (JCP).

[c] In November 1955, the Liberal Democratic party (LDP) was established, absorbing the former Liberal and Democratic parties.

[d] In October 1955, the left and right wing Socialist parties amalgamated, later absorbing the Workers-Farmers party too, forming the Japan Socialist party (JSP).

[e] In 1960, certain factions split from the Japan Socialist party to establish the Democratic Socialist party (DSP).

[f] Originally organized as the political arm of the lay Buddhist organization known as Soka Gakkai, this group was formally organized as a political party in 1966.

urbanized the environment, the less salient are age, education level and indeed occupation as determining factors of party support (see Table 4-9). Since the urban sector of Japan has expanded strikingly in recent years, these facts suggest a decline in party loyalty and a possible increase in the floating vote. A second explanation is to be found in the fact that certain of the "modern" groups, especially the young and the highly educated, are showing an increasing propensity not to vote at all, thereby weakening proportionately the reformist parties. This nonvoting tendency would seem to be related to the spread of certain postindustrial values exemplified by the preference for living one's life "to suit one's taste" which, we have seen, is displacing older values of social discipline.

But perhaps the single most important explanation for the continued strength of the LDP and the growth in importance of the Kōmei and Communist parties, are the growing strength of organization in those parties and the relative weakness of such organization in the Japan Socialist Party (JSP) and the Democratic Socialist Party (DSP). The traditional party in Japan, true to its nineteenth-century origins, had been an organization of officeholders and local notables, having little or no mass base. After World War II, these loose elitist groups which had their counterparts in the traditional order were challenged by more highly-organized parties who sought mass membership on the model of the Socialist and Marxist-Leninist parties of the West. The Japan Communist party went farthest along this path and is today the most highly-organized of all Japanese parties, increasing its dues-paying membership from about 20,000 in 1955 to 300,000 today and building up its daily party newspaper distribution to nearly two million copies.[6]

All other parties have felt the magnetism of this model, but none has been able to duplicate it. Memberships in the Japan Socialist party and the Democratic Socialist party remain extremely low (35,000 and 50,000 respectively).[7] For organizational strength they have come to rely, somewhat in

Table 4-9
Correlation between Occupation, Age, Educational Level, and Party Support, 1971

	Occupation	Age	Educational Level
Rural Area (gunbu)	0.470	0.227	0.140
Small Cities	0.460	0.260	0.181
Middle Cities	0.477	0.251	0.046
Seven Big Cities	0.287	0.114	0.124
Setagaya Ward in Tokyo	0.129	0.095	0.114

Notes: Figures for the upper four rows are computed from the original data in the survey made by Kōmei Senkyo Renmei of the 1971 House of Councilors election.

The figures are square roots of Crammer's contingency coefficients. Party support is regrouped into two categories: LDP vs. JSP, DSP, and JCP.

the manner of the British Labour party, on what Maurice Duverger calls "indirect structures,"[8] that is, on two national federations of labor unions, the JSP on Sōhyō with its four million members and the DSP on Dōmei with its two million members. The Kōmei party has another kind of indirect structure, the Sōka Gakkai [value creation society], which is a lay association of the Nichiren Shōshu Buddhist sect with five million members.[9]

Among the conservatives the response to the need for stable party support has taken a different form, that of building personal sponsoring associations, not for the Liberal Democratic party as such, but for each individual conservative politician in his own district. Since the formation of the party in 1955 the number of these associations, known as kōenkai, has grown dramatically until now they are estimated to embrace about 17.2 percent of the party's supporters or about 4.5 million people and to have contacted possibly 20 or 30 million more.[10] Through such associations, the conservative politicians now gather and distribute benefits, the latter ranging from the soliciting of governmental funds for local public works to arranging for university admissions or jobs for children of constituents. The kōenkai serve social and recreational functions too: they organize sight-seeing tours, for example, and sponsor bowling matches. The interesting thing is that these organizations do not resemble mass parties of the West European types; there is, for example, no clear definition of membership and no clear concentration on issues, the organizational principle being personal loyalty to the particular politician concerned.[11] In this latter regard they are distinguished also from the American-type party in which affiliation, loose though it is, in most cases survives a change in leadership. It has been suggested that the relationship between an LDP politician and his *kōenkai* members is similar to the patron-client relationship found in groups in developing societies.[12] But the *kōenkai* often includes a vast number of people under its umbrella, the largest reportedly embracing about 50,000 persons;[13] moreover, the relationship between the politician and the *kōenkai* members is more tenuous and organizational than one usually finds in groups in developing societies. If this is clientelism, it is organizational clientelism.

The growth of these peculiarly Japanese forms of political organization, generating as they do intense competition within the party, has been condemned by the LDP's central leadership almost from the beginning. In 1963, for example, these organizations were severely faulted for "concentrating on activities centered on particular individuals and hindering activities of the party."[14] The solution, it was felt, was gradually to absorb them into the party organization, in the beginning by requiring that influential members and at least 500 members of each be registered in local branches of the party. The effort was made and by the summer of 1971, 800,000 persons from the local sponsoring associations were reported to have been registered.[15] But the results have been disappointing. Once registered, few remained in the party to pay their dues for even an additional year. The reason seems to have been that the lists of 500 persons from each personal sponsoring association were drawn up often without the consent of the persons involved and the dues for the first year were usually paid by the politician concerned, not by the *kōenkai* members.

Not only have the conservative *kōenkai* not been absorbed into the LDP, but their strength is growing. According to recent surveys, the percentage of the electorate who acknowledge membership in a *kōenkai* rose from 5.8 percent in 1967 to 11.5 percent in 1970 to 13.7 percent in 1971.[16]

Thus, except for the Japan Communist party, the highly organized mass party which so caught the imagination of many Japanese during the industrial era never actually caught on. The Socialists remain dependent on their unions, and efforts to encourage labor union members to affiliate directly with the party have resulted usually in the addition of "sleeping members" who nominally register, but drop out within a year or two. The Kōmei party, which in 1970 separated itself from its own "indirect structure," the Sōka Gakkai, found it could attract very few members who were not from the Gakkai. Without the direct backup of the Gakkai as in the past, it suffered a striking defeat in the December 1972 election. And the Liberal Democratic party is more and more dependent on its personal sponsoring associations. Clearly, Japan's traditional paternalistic behavior patterns and values proved to be remarkably adaptable to the demands generated by industrial society and there is every reason to believe that they will survive in the politics of the postindustrial age.

On the other hand, the emergence of certain postindustrial values also is not without effect. Citizens' participation, for example, has been more and more highly valued. The result has not been the reinvigoration of existing political parties, but the emergence of nonpartisan citizens' movements around various issues such as environmental protection, educational improvement, and the promotion of welfare. Local governments have been more susceptible than the central government to such demands. As a matter of fact, a political style emphasizing citizens' participation has become more and more popular among the candidates running for the office of governor or mayor. Recently in local elections, especially in big cities, candidates supported by the LDP who emphasize the importance of their ties with the governing party and the central government have been losing with unexpectedly large margins to candidates backed by the opposition parties who emphasize the importance of citizens' participation. A good example is Ryokichi Minobe's gubernatorial election in Tokyo in 1971.

Another recent change is the increasing importance of the personalities of the candidates. Of course, personality has always counted in Japanese elections; however, recently a fluctuation in the votes according to the attractiveness of the candidates has become particularly pronounced. The electoral success of Minobe is at least partly attributable to his famous smile and glamorous personality.

The persistence of older values and structures side by side with the emergence of new forms of political participation and new appeals of political candidates, makes prediction of the future of Japanese politics very uncertain. It is possible that the LDP may lose its majority in the House of Councilors by the next regular election in 1974. The Communists, in turn, may be able to continue their advance, possibly securing 20 percent of the votes and seats and acquiring thereby the capability of creating more noisy parliamentary sessions and even paralyzing the Diet. But what would follow if the LSP should lose its majority in the Diet—which party would benefit most or which parties or factions would form the succeeding coalition—is impossible to foresee.

The impact of the postindustrialism on the bureaucracy also is ambiguous. On the one hand, it would seem to strengthen the bureaucracy. In spite of the postwar reforms under the American occupation, the Japanese bureaucracy, especially in comparison with that in the United States, has remained strongly centralized and powerful. These characteristics give it an advantage in utilizing the improvement of informational techniques for elaborate and sophisticated planning. The Japanese bureaucracy has long been able to get meticulous statistical data from local bodies simply by circulating orders or notices. Now various ministries of the central government are competing in introducing high-level techniques for storing and retrieving the data thus gathered. The Ministry of Labor, for example, as early as 1964 established a huge computerized center for the labor market, capable of storing and retrieving the information gathered from labor stabilization offices throughout the country. The Ministry of Construction is trying to establish a territorial information center, where detailed information on regional development all over Japan will be stored and retrieved.

The bureaucracy is strengthened also by the expansion of the national budget, made possible by the growth of the economy and the concomitant "natural increase" of governmental revenues through taxes. As GNP has doubled every five years, the governmental budget also has doubled every five years, growing eight times between 1955 and 1970. Of course, the budget is determined by the Diet; however, it is the bureaucrats who draft the budget and it is the bureaucrats who administer the ever-growing expenditures.

One of the reasons for the bureaucracy's ability to adapt to the new postindustrial forces has been the existence of an elite corps within it. By "elite corps" I mean not only those who are presently occupying top positions in the bureaucracy, but also those junior bureaucrats who have passed certain categories of higher civil service examinations. They exist as a semiformally recognized group with high solidarity and interaction within each ministry. The practice is to give them special privileges of fast promotion and careful training. Although recruitment is based on open examination, the number of annual recruits is carefully limited. For instance, in the Ministry of International Trade and Industry with 12,000 personnel, around twenty new graduates from the universities are accepted annually in this capacity, that is, as new members of its elite corps, which numbers about four hundred or so. Early selection, careful training, planned rotation and fast promotion work in general to maintain a high capability and morale.

But the future of the bureaucracy is no more certain than that of the parties, for other forces are at work to weaken and change it. For one thing, its present position rests in part on close cooperation with the LDP majority in the Diet. If this majority should be replaced by a multiparty coalition, one result might be political immobility and a clear opportunity for the bureaucracy to gain more influence as an independent, stabilizing power; but, alternatively, it is also possible that in such a circumstance the various partners of the coalition would approach the bureaucracy separately and competitively, causing it to lose the unity fostered hitherto by close association with the LDP.

Secondly, it may be challenged by increasing local initiative. The emerging emphasis on participatory values has been felt especially in local bodies of urban and suburban areas. As mentioned above, often the successful gubernatorial or mayoral candidates are those who encourage citizens' participation and demand more decentralization of governmental power. Under these new leaders, local governments tend to follow a different line from that of the national government. Thus, even if the LDP were able to maintain its majority in the Diet and even if the national bureaucracy were able to retain its powerful position at the center, an emerging friction between the national and local governments may well operate to counter the bureaucracy's centralized and sophisticated planning from above. Thus the triangle of the LDP, bureaucracy, and big business which has been so powerful up to now may in the future meet more and more resistance from a loose tripartite coalition of opposition parties, urban local governments and citizens' movements—a counter force which might gain particular strength should the LDP lose its majority in the Diet.

Thirdly, it may be doubted whether the elite core of the Japanese national bureaucracy can survive as presently constituted. The discriminatory system on which the elite corps is based may shortly find itself in difficulty. So far, the bureaucracy has tried successfully to limit the recruitment of university graduates to the elite corps, filling the bulk of its nonelite jobs with older persons and female high school graduates. Were this practice to continue, it would result in the lowering of the quality of the nonelite sector of the national bureaucracy. In any event, with the spread of higher education, the pressure is on for the national bureaucracy to accept a far larger number of university graduates than has been its practice. If this change is made, university graduates will need to be appointed to what have been thought of as nonelite as well as elite positions, making it increasingly difficult to preserve the uniqueness of the elite corps. The solution for this would seem to be to open the gate wide to university graduates and let them compete on the job. Actually, local governments are already doing this; for instance, the Tokyo metropolitan government alone has been hiring more university graduates annually than the total number recruited annually for the elite corps of the entire national bureaucracy. The present elite corps, of course, is reluctant to make such a reform which would result in the dissolution of its privileged status and the loss of its special training, with the possible effect of lowering the bureaucracy's effectiveness. The LDP also is opposed since it is fused with the elite corps through personal ties and the mutual exchange of benefits. But the time is not far distant when such a reform will have to be considered, either because of pressure from other political parties with which the LDP is forced to bargain to form a coalition or because of acute labor unrest provoked by the present discriminatory system.

Why, in comparison with the speed and the scale of change in Japan's economy and consumption style, have changes in the political sphere been so gradual? The truth is that not only in politics, but in all areas of society which are deeply imbued with norms and values, changes do not come quickly unless there has been forced indoctrination or brainwashing. The widespread acceptance of new values usually requires a generational change. Meanwhile, old values persist. It should not be surprising, therefore, that in Japan, where 40 percent of the people were engaged in agriculture as late as 1955, the traditional communal values nourished in the agrarian village remain strong.

Accordingly, just as Japan was a latecomer to the industrial age, so will it be later than the United States and West European countries in fully entering the period of postindustrialization. The extended implication of this is a time-lag theory. With the passing of time, gradually the "traditional" and "industrial" values will be more and more sloughed off and "postindustrial" values will in the main take over; and only sometime later will the politics of Japan come gradually to resemble the politics of other postindustrial societies in Western Europe and the United States.

But this resemblance is apt to be slow not only in coming but in the end incomplete. One must recognize the viable nature of certain Japanese traditional norms and values and the dexterity of the Japanese elites in utilizing them, as they did, for nation-building and industrialization in the prewar period and for reconstruction and economic growth in the postwar period. Lifelong employment and the seniority wage system, for example, are still being practiced even after the rise of fairly strong labor unions. *Ringisei,* often translated as "decision-making from below" or "consensus decision-making" is an established practice in Japanese organizational decision-making, in which the plans are drawn up by the middle-echelon and circulated upward successively through a number of officeholders in the heirarchy of organization for approval. *Nemawashi* is the practice of informal consultation to get the approval of the people concerned in advance of presenting a formal proposal.[17] These and other practices, the origins of which can be traced far back in traditional Japanese cultural patterns, still survive and function in the most modern Japanese private enterprise or governmental bureaucracy. As mentioned above, LDP politicians have built up expensive but effective political vote-getting organizations of mass clientelism. At least so far, these traditional practices have worked well in the modern context. Who is to say that they or other traditional values and practices will not prove equally adaptable to the needs of the postindustrial age? And to the extent that such cultural differences, deriving from different historical heritages, continue to distinguish one society from another, postindustrial politics in Japan will remain quite different from those in either the United States or Western Europe, in spite of the similarity or even identity of their stages of economic development and their common features as free societies.

Finally, political change in Japan has been retarded also by the continuation of the LDP in power since 1955. Were it to lose its majority in the Diet, there would suddenly open a completely new epoch in Japanese politics, possibly releasing economic and social energies now pent up and causing chain reactions in the political sphere. However this might speed up political change, the overwhelming majority of Japanese opinion leaders believe—as do I—that Japan is very unlikely to abandon its democratic institutions or negate its democratic values.[18]

Notes

1. See J. C. Abegglen, *The Japanese Factory: Aspects of its Social Organization* (Glencoe: Free Press, 1958).

2. This question was originally designed in 1930. It was used in surveys of twenty-year-old male military conscripts in 1930 and 1940. To secure a time-series comparison, the Institute of Mathematical Statistics asked this again in 1953 and has been asking it in repeated surveys since then.

3. See Ronald Inglehart, "The Silent Revolution in Europe: Intergenerational Change in Post-Industrial Societies," *American Political Science Review*, 65, no. 4 (December 1971), 991-1017. In this paper, Inglehart tries to prove the emergence of "post-industrial values" in six West

European societies based on cross-national surveys. The indicator which he used in measuring postindustrial values was the choice of participation and freedom of speech over order and concern with rising prices. No comparable survey has been conducted in Japan and the United States. The question about how one should live his life was not originally designed to measure postindustrial values and is used as an indicator here only because a better one specifically designed for the purpose is not yet available.

4. See, for example, the author's essay on the "Pattern of Politics in Present Day Japan," written in 1963 and published in S.M. Lipset and Stein Rokkan, eds., *Party Systems and Voter Alignments* (New York: The Free Press, 1967), pp. 447-66.

5. A report by the author to the annual meeting of the Japan Political Science Association, November 14, 1972, using data from a nationwide survey conducted by the Institute of International Relations, Sophia University, on "International Attitudes of the Japanese People."

6. Kotaro Tawara, *Hadaka no Nihon Kyosanto* [The Japan Communist party unmasked] (Tokyo: Nisshinhodo Shuppanbu, 1972), pp. 17-28.

7. As of August 1971. From *Yomiuri Nenkan, 1972.* [Yomiuri yearbook, 1972].

8. Maurice Duverger, *Political Parties* (London: Methuen, 1964), pp. 5-16.

9. *Soka Gakkai* itself boasts that it has 7.5 million *households* as its members. However, outside observers and analysts agree that this is an inflated figure. According to the common understanding among them, a membership of 4 or 5 million would be closer to the reality. See James W. White, *The Sokagakkai and Mass Society* (Stanford: Stanford University Press, 1970), pp. 57-61.

10. Komei Senkyo Renmei, *Dai 7-kai toitsu-chihosenkyo to yukensha* [7th Unified Local Elections and the Voter], II, 1972, 206.

11. For a detailed analysis of *koenkai,* see Gerald L. Curtis, *Election Campaigning Japanese Style* (New York: Columbia University Press, 1971), ch. 5.

12. See James C. Scott, "Patron-Client Politics and Political Change in Southeast Asia," in *American Political Science Review,* 66, no. 1: 91-113.

13. *Election Campaigning Japanese Style*, p. 130.

14. Proposals by the Subcommittee on Organization, October 15, 1963.

15. Jiyu Minshuto Zenkoku Soshiki Iinkai, *Soshiki kyoka no ayumi* [Progress report on strengthening the party organization], (Jiyu Minshuto, 1971), p. 3.

16. From surveys by Komei Senkyo Renmei.

17. See Kiyoaki Tsuji, "Decision-Making in the Japanese Government: A Study of Ringisei," in Robert E. Ward, ed., *Political Development in Modern Japan* (Princeton: Princeton University Press, 1968), pp. 457-75.

18. According to a survey of Japanese opinion leaders by mail questionnaire, less than 4 percent of them foresee the downfall of democracy in Japan in the future. Yasumasa Tanaka, Ken'ichi Koyama and Hisaaki Yasuda *Nihon no kokka mokuhyo ni kansuru chosa* [A survey of national goals of Japan: an interim report], July 1972, p. 11.

Chapter Five

Postindustrial Politics: How Different Will It Be?

Samuel P. Huntington

The concept of postindustrial society was advanced in the early 1960s by Daniel Bell as a model of society comparable to, but significantly different from, those of industrial and agrarian society. In the following decade, the concept was elaborated by Bell, reformulated by others, and relabeled by some.[1] Individual postindustrial society theorists stress different aspects of the concept, but they would generally agree on the following as central elements distinguishing postindustrial from industrial and agrarian society:

1. The economic predominance of the service sector in contrast to that of the industrial and agricultural sectors
2. The predominance in the labor force of white-collar in contrast to blue-collar workers and, particularly, the large size and critical role in the economy of professional, technical, and managerial workers

3. A central role in the economy and society of theoretical knowledge, technology, research and development in contrast to physical capital and consequently the central role of institutions such as universities, think tanks, and media, which—in contrast to factories—are devoted to the creation and transmission of information
4. High and widespread levels of economic well-being and affluence, leading to increased leisure for the bulk of the population, with a few isolated "pockets" of poverty, in contrast to a small well-off elite and widespread poverty
5. Higher levels of education for the bulk of the population with a college education becoming the norm, in contrast to a norm of primary education
6. A new "post-bourgeois" value structure concerned with the quality of life and humanistic values, in contrast to a "Protestant" inner-directed work ethic

Theorists of postindustrial society thus define it primarily by its economic, social, and, in part, cultural characteristics. They do not give a central role to the nature of its political institutions, political processes, political rulers, or political values. To a considerable degree, indeed, the postindustrial society concept is not a political concept at all. It thus contrasts with other models of society such as the concepts of oriental despotism or totalitarianism, which stress the role of the state in society, and with models such as Lasswell's garrison state, which assign a central role to the nature of the rulers and the mechanisms of rule. Brzezinski devotes substantial attention to politics, but a majority of his ten contrasts between industrial and technetronic society are nonpolitical; so also are all of Bell's five dimensions of postindustrial society; Kahn and Wiener's list of fifteen characteristics of postindustrial society has only one which is even vaguely political and that one ("erosion of 'national interest' values?") is the only one followed by a question mark![2] Conceivably a postindustrial society may have some distinctive political characteristics, but, if so, they presumably derive from its central socioeconomic characteristics; they are not themselves a part of the essence of such a society.

Not only is postindustrial society not defined in political terms, but, by and large, those who have defined it in other terms have not elaborated at length the political implications of their concept. The concept, according to Bell, "does not deal with the political and cultural dimension of society" and "can say little about the nature of political crises" which may occur. Bell does, however, suggest that a major problem in postindustrial society will be the management of the relations between the bureaucratic decisionmakers in economic, social, and political organizations and those who are excluded from decision-making. Bell also points to the shift in power from legislative to executive organs and the "loss of insulating space" as a result of media and communications developments which multiply tremendously the impact which any one event has throughout the society. Professional and technical experts clearly play a more important role in postindustrial society. Hence power will increasingly come to be based on control of skill (access to which is gained by education) rather than by control of property (acquired by inheritance or entrepreneurial ability) or political office (acquired by co-optation or mobilizing a following). Still, when critical decisions are to be made, it is, nonetheless, "not the technocrat who ultimately holds power, but the politician."[3]

In somewhat similar fashion, Brzezinski also sees the plutocratic power-wielders of industrial society challenged in technetronic society by "political leadership, which is itself permeated by individuals possessing special skills and intellectual talents. Knowledge becomes a tool of power and the effective mobilization of talent an important way to acquire power." In this society the problems of arranging for political participation become increasingly difficult and "political alienation" hence more persuasive. The mass media make it possible for "magnetic and attractive personalities" to command the attention and mobilize the support of "millions of unorganized citizens." On the one hand, the citizen is drawn into politics; on the other, his feelings of impotence and of the futility of politics escalate.[4]

Beyond these suggestive comments, little systematic attention seems to have been devoted to the nature of postindustrial politics. There are three possible reasons for this. First, it is possible that politics will simply be rather unimportant in postindustrial society. The concept of postindustrial society with its emphasis on knowledge, rationality, and technology has certain resemblances to other essentially nonpolitical utopias and models of society where "the governing of men is replaced by the administration of things." As these words suggest, such models have an ancient and honorable intellectual history. They are the product of man's hope to transcend the irrationalities of conflict and power. Earlier ages sought such escape through religion and mysticism. The nineteenth and twentieth centuries have sought it by means of science, technology, and economic affluence. In some measure, the concept of postindustrial society, as it has been developed, appears to be heir to this tradition. Interestingly, Christopher Lasch, a radical commentator on the postindustrial society, also sees it in a neo-Marxian image, but instead of seeing it distinguished by those features which Marx saw in postcapitalist society, he instead sees it as manifesting in more intense form the contradictions which Marx ascribed to the capitalist society.[5]

A second reason why postindustrial society theorists do not focus on politics could be because they see no significant difference between industrial and postindustrial politics. The economy, occupational structure, educational levels, lifestyles, role of knowledge and technology, may differ drastically from one to the other, but conceivably these could have little effect on politics. Here the assumption of discontinuity between economy and society, on the one hand, and politics on the other, would be decidedly un-Marxian. This may, however, be what Bell is suggesting when he says that individual postindustrial societies "will have different political and cultural configurations."[6] If this is indeed the case, then politics will be insulated from socioeconomic change and will reflect its own dynamics.

Finally, postindustrial politics could be neglected not because it is unimportant or undifferent but simply because it is unpleasant. In this respect, there may be a distinct contrast in the evaluations implicitly attached to postindustrial society, on the one hand, and its politics, on the other. By and large, the theorists of postindustrial society have viewed its emergence positively; it will, after all, be a society of greater affluence and education in which theoretical knowledge and technology have central roles. Conceivably, however, the politics of postindustrialism and particularly of the transition to postindustrialism could be less benign. A more rationalized society could generate less rational political conflict, with politics becoming the arena for the expression of emotional frustration and irrational impulse, which find little outlet in society. Postindustrial politics, in short, could be the darker side of postindustrial society.

Given the relative lack of attention which they have received, how can one go about delineating the major characteristics of postindustrial politics, particularly with reference to their manifestation in the United States? Three approaches are possible. First, if the politics of a society bears some definite and intimate relationship to the rest of society, it ought to be possible to deduce the principal political features of postindustrial society from the economic-social-cultural characteristics of that society. Much has been written on the latter; a little active deduction should supply the former. Most of what postindustrial society theorists have written about postindustrial politics has indeed been derived in this manner. Second, if it is assumed that the United States is an emerging postindustrial society, it ought to be possible to project into the future recent American political trends which seem to be related to that evolution. What, in short, are the political trends which parallel increasing affluence, education, white-collar work, and the like?

Finally, if it is assumed that the transition from industrial to postindustrial society is comparable to the transition from agrarian to industrial society, it ought to be possible to reason by analogy from what is known about the process and result of one transition to what is likely to happen in the subsequent transition. The validity of these approaches, it should be noted, in each case rests on the validity of one particular, highly debatable assumption. Consequently, eclecticism and the use of all three approaches would seem to be very much in order. A political development which is suggested by all three approaches would, it may be assumed, have a reasonably strong likelihood of materializing. Deduction and projection are reasonably familiar approaches to this type of problem; the ways in which analogy may be used, however, require some further elaboration.

According to the analogic approach, explanations of political change in the agrarian-to-industrial transition should be suggestive in understanding the political aspects of the shift from industrial to postindustrial society. Three general explanations have dominated the analysis of the political aspects of modernization from traditional (agrarian) to modern (industrial) society.

The *level of development* explanation relates political values, processes, and institutions to the level of socioeconomic development in the society. This approach is found in its most explicit form in the argument that higher levels of socioeconomic development produce higher levels of political democracy. Its implications for postindustrial politics are: (a) that change from industrial to postindustrial society will involve fundamental changes in politics; and (b) that if political democracy is the dominant political form associated with industrial society, the political system prevalent in postindustrial society should be as far removed from political democracy as the latter was from the oligarchical or autocratic systems of rule found in preindustrial agrarian societies. Critics of this approach argue that there is no necessary relationship between political systems and

94

socioeconomic development. The exceptions and overlap in this presumed correlation, they say, are so great as virtually to rob it of meaning. Hence the implication that there should be marked differences between the political system of the most advanced postindustrial society and that of the average industrial society is a rather dubious one.

The *starting point* theory argues that the political system which emerges from the process of industrialization will in large part be shaped by the political system existing when the society was in its traditional phase and began the process of rapid socioeconomic change. In its bluntest form, this theory argues that feudal or, more broadly, pluralist traditional political systems usually end up with pluralist and democratic modern political systems, while societies with centralized, autocratic, and bureaucratic traditional political systems usually end up with autocratic and totalitarian modern political systems. The implication of this theory for the shift to postindustrial society is that postindustrial politics will reflect the political systems of societies in their industrial phase. Hence the politics of postindustrial United States and Japan will have significant differences, but these will pale before the differences between these systems and the political system of the postindustrial Soviet Union.

A third approach stresses the nature of the *transitional process*. Was it prolonged or rapid, early or late? What was the sequence of change? Was it peaceful or violent? Differences in these aspects of the transition lead to more or less political stability and more or less democracy in the outcome. The evidence to support the transitional process argument with respect to the political systems of industrialized societies is fairly strong. The problem in applying it to the emergence of postindustrial society Is that the key characteristics or turning points in the transition to that form of society are rather hard to pin down. In the earlier transition, for instance, it is tremendously important for the future of a society whether its middle class first develops in the countryside or in the city. What is the equivalent for the shift to postindustrial society? The process of transition to postindustrialism appears to be brief and also remains rather vague.

The seeming parallels in the movement from agrarian to industrial and from industrial to postindustrial society are suggestive. The conclusions which one draws from these parallels, however, will differ significantly according to the relative weight which is assigned to the level of development, starting point, and transitional process explanations. All three explanations seem to have some usefulness in illuminating aspects of the earlier transition. If one had to make a rough judgment, however, one would have to conclude that by and large the transitional process explanation was probably the most useful of the three, the starting point approach the next most generally useful, with the level of development thesis following in third place. If this should also be true of the movement from industrial to postindustrial society, it is desirable to spell out more explicitly the process of change.

Theorists of modernization have stressed the long transitional phase in the evolution from traditional agrarian society to modern industrial society. They think in terms of a threefold sequence of traditional, transitional, modern. In a pioneering discussion of this transition, Karl Deutsch identified seven key indicators (e.g., literacy, per capita income, urbanization, mass-media audience, nonagricultural employment) of the process of "social mobilization" by which societies moved out of the traditional phase. In the shifts along these various dimensions, he suggested the possibility of "critical" thresholds at which "significant changes" occur in the political and other side effects of the process.[7]

Theorists of postindustrial society have dealt much more concretely with the components of that society than they have with the nature and length of the transition to that society. In general, the assumption often seems to be that the transition will be a brief one. The postindustrial Athena appropriately springs full-grown from the brow of the industrial Zeus. Alternatively, postindustrial society itself may be seen as a society in transition, as a society in which the trends toward the six conditions which define the postindustrial type play a dominant role. By and large, there appears to be general agreement that the United States is now well into the transition from industrial to postindustrial society and that Sweden and some other Western European counties are not far behind. Both Bell and Lasch see the "birth years" of postindustrial society in the United States in the immediate aftermath of World War II.[8]

During the twenty years after World War II, many of the social trends toward postindustrial society did pass what might be considered critical thresholds dividing postindustrial from industrial society. In the United States, there was a "shift from a predominantly industrial to a predominantly service economy shortly after World War II," with over 50 percent of the labor force first being recorded in service industries in 1950 (see Table 5-1).[9] Canada apparently passed this mark in 1958, the United Kingdom in 1965, and Belgium, Netherlands, and Sweden in 1970. Japan and France appear to go over this threshold by the end of the 1970s. A society may also pass a benchmark on the road to postindustrialism when the number of white-collar workers in its labor force

Table 5-1
Percentage Distribution of Civilian Employment by Sector

	1940	1950	1960	1970
Agriculture[a]	18.8	12.3	8.5	4.5
Industry[b]	30.0	33.7	33.4	33.2
Services[c]	49.7	54.0	58.1	62.3

[a]Includes also forestry, hunting, and fishing.

[b]Includes manufacturing, mining, construction.

[c]Includes transportation, communication, public utilities, trade, finance, public administration, private household services, and miscellaneous services.

Source: Constance Serrentino, "Comparing Employment Shifts in 10 Industrialized Countries," *Monthly Labor Review* 94 (October 1971), pp. 4-7, for 1950-1970. U.S. Bureau of the Census; *Statistical Abstract of the United States: 1942* (Washington, D.C., 64th ed., 1943), pp. 66-67, for 1940.

exceeds the number of blue-collar workers. In the United States the blue-collar share of the labor force reached its peak in 1950 with 41.1 percent of the total. By 1970 it had dropped to 35.3 percent; by 1980 it is estimated that it will be 32.7 percent. The white-collar proportion, on the other hand, has risen steadily from 31 percent of the total in 1940 to 48.3 percent in 1970 and will pass 50 percent by 1980. The number of white-collar workers exceeded the number of blue-collar workers for the first time in 1956 (see Table 5-2).

Another postindustrial trend is, of course, the rising level of formal education (see Table 5-3). A significant threshold here might be the point at which 40 percent or more of the relevant age groups attend college. In the United States that level appears to have been reached about 1963.[10] An alternative threshold might be the point where 25 percent or more of the adult population has attended college, a mark which the United States should pass in the mid-1970s. Another important benchmark indicative of the relative importance of the "knowledge industry" is the proportion of the gross national product which is spent on research and development. In the United States this ratio rose steadily during the 1950s and early 1960s, passing the 2.5 percent mark in 1959.[11] Finally, the shift in the location of people is equally likely to have significant implications, political and otherwise. Before World War II only a small fraction of the population lived in the suburban portions of metropolitan areas. By 1970, this percentage had increased to 37.2 percent, and it is likely that by 1980 about half the American people will be suburbanites (see Table 5-4). Between 1960 and 1970 the population of central cities grew by only 1 percent, while that of the surrounding suburban areas grew by 28 percent.

All in all these various indicators suggest that if the concept of postindustrial society does have useful meaning, the United States did indeed start the transition into that phase immediately after World War II with this transition manifesting itself dramatically in the distribution of the labor force among sectors and in the composition of the labor force, and

Table 5-2
Percentage Distribution of Labor Force by Occupation

	1940	1950	1960	1970	1980 est.
White-collar	31.0	36.6	43.4	48.3	50.8
Blue-collar	40.0	41.1	36.6	35.3	32.7
Service	11.7	10.4	12.2	12.4	13.8
Farmers	17.3	11.7	7.9	4.0	2.7

Sources: Calculated by James R. Kurth from series D72-122, *Historical Statistics of the United States from Colonial Times to 1957*, p. 74 (Data 1900-1950); *Manpower Report of the President*, 1971, pp. 215-216, 297 (Data 1960-1980). Data for 1950 and before are not fully comparable to data for 1960 and after.

Table 5-3
Percentage Distribution of Population by Education

	1940	1950	1960	1970	1980 est.
Adults 25 and older who have					
completed high school	24.5	34.3	41.1	55.2	65.4
attended college		13.2	16.5	21.2	27.3
completed 4 years of					
college	4.6	6.2	7.7	11.0	14.8
Youth who are students					
age 18-19		29.4	38.4	47.7	
20-24		9.0	13.1	21.5	

Sources: U.S. Bureau of the Census, *Statistical Abstract of the United States: 1970* (Washington, D.C., 91st ed., 1970), pp. 108, 112; Ibid.: 1972, 93rd ed., pp. 109, 111, 112.

Table 5-4
Percentage Distribution of Population by Residence

	1950	1960	1970	1980 est.
Central cities	34.7	32.3	31.4	25
Suburban areas	24.6	30.9	37.2	50
Outside metropolitan areas	40.8	36.7	31.4	25

Source: U.S. Bureau of the Census, *Statistical Abstract of the United States: 1970*, 91st ed., p. 16; Ibid.: 1972, 93rd ed., p. 16.

then in changes in residential patterns and levels of education. At this point, it is clearly still too early to identify the critical thresholds in these trends, passage over which triggers significant ramifications in other areas of society. If, however, one wants to pick out certain possible critical thresholds, then the progress of the United States into post-industrialism could be marked as follows:

Possible Critical Thresholds	Year
1. 50 of labor force in service sector	1948
2. 25 of population in suburbs	1950
3. More white-collar than blue-collar workers	1956
4. 2.5 of GNP devoted to R & D	1959
5. 40 of relevant age group in college	1963
6. 25 of adult population attended college	1976
7. 50 of labor force white-collar workers	1980
8. 50 of population in suburbs	1980
9. 50 of relevant age group in college	1980?

The percentages of the labor force employed in industry and in blue-collar occupations both peaked in 1950. Consequently, the process of transition out of industrial society may be appropriately dated from that time. Assuming that estimates of future trends hold up, the transition to postindustrialism can perhaps be said to end about 1980, when 50 percent of the labor force will be in white-collar employment, 50 percent of the population will live in suburbs, and possibly 50 percent of the college-age group will be in college.

The most important political consequence of the shift from agrarian to industrial society, it is commonly argued, was the significant expansion of the politically relevant classes in the population and the resulting expansion of political participation. Differences in levels of political participation constitute the most critical political difference between traditional and modern society. Modernization and industrialization change the distribution of social statuses in society and the level of organizational complexity of the society. Higher levels of socioeconomic status and greater degrees of organizational involvement generate more political participation. Among the relevant status variables, the most influential is education. The population of a postindustrial society will have extremely high levels of education, with a substantial portion of the population having attended college and an overwhelming majority being high-school graduates. If the relationships between educational status and political participation which have previously prevailed within the United States remain unchanged, the levels of political participation in the United States should go up significantly. The tendencies in this direction should be reinforced by the higher levels of affluence and more leisure time. In addition, the steady increase in home ownership (part of the process of increasing affluence and suburbanization) should also promote greater political activity.

In the development of the United States, the achievement of almost universal white male literacy occurred simultaneously with the tremendous expansion in political participation and interest of the Jacksonian period. At the same time there was also a great increase in newspaper circulation and other forms of communication. Political involvement and voting participation remained high until the end of the nineteenth century, when a combination of factors, primarily political in character, produced a steady decline in voting participation which was not significantly reversed until the New Deal period. By and large, this overall decline in voting participation was concentrated among southern blacks, lower-class groups, and, after women's suffrage, among women. In Europe, the emergence of industrial society produced high levels of class consciousness among lower-class groups and hence high levels of voting participation by such groups. In the United States, industrial society emerged in such a manner as to abort the development of class-consciousness and hence was associated with a decline in

101

voting participation by lower-status groups. Consequently, with the emergence of industrial society in the United States, voting participation came to be very closely associated with socioeconomic status, more so, probably, than in any other democratic society.

The emergence of a postindustrial society will disseminate more broadly throughout the population those status characteristics which are associated with voting and other forms of political participation. In the 1968 presidential election, for instance, the overall turnout was 61.8 percent, but the reported turnout of those who had attended college was 81.2 percent while that of those who had not gone beyond high school was 72.5 percent and that of those who had not gone beyond grade school was only 54.5 percent.[12] A society in which almost everyone has completed high school and many have gone to college would, presumably, have voting participation rates of 75 to 80 percent instead of the 55 to 60 percent rates which have characterized American politics during its industrial phase. In addition, voting itself is less highly correlated to socioeconomic status than other forms of political participation such as partisan activity in addition to voting and cooperative action with others in politically-oriented organizations.[13] Thus, because the shift to postindustrial society involves significant status enhancement for large portions of the population, postindustrial society, *particularly in the United States,* should be characterized by much higher levels of political participation than obtained in industrial society.

Because the white-collar, better-educated, suburban people are more involved in politics than most other groups, the numerical political impact of these people runs ahead of their simple numerical growth. The political sphere, in a sense, becomes the first register of more far-reaching social change. The political manifestations of the emergence of postindustrial society are well revealed in the Harris survey data on the proportions which the relevant groups contributed to the voting turnouts in the 1968 and 1972 presidential elections. Union members cast 23 percent of the vote in 1968, but only 18 percent four years later. The suburban share of the total vote, on the other hand, went up from 27 to 33 percent of the total. The votes cast by those with no more than a grade-school education amounted to 19 percent of the total in 1968 and 13 percent in 1972. The votes of the college-educated, in contrast, went up from 27 to 35 percent of the total. The vote of those earning between $5,000 and $10,000 a year dropped from 43 percent of the total in 1968 to 33 percent of the total in 1972; on the other hand, the vote of those earning $15,000 or more went up from 11 percent to 20 percent. All in all, during this four-year period, the proportion of the vote cast by those rising social forces characteristic of postindustrial society increased from roughly 45 percent of the total to about 50 percent of the total. As Louis Harris put it, the Silent Majority is a shrinking majority, and a "new coalition for change" is displacing it on the national political scene.[14]

In the transition from agrarian to industrial society, the expansion of political participation often occurred too rapidly and too disconnectedly to permit the adaptation of traditional political institutions or the development of political institutions to provide appropriate channels and structures for that participation. Where this happened—where the institutions for participation, primarily parties and electoral systems, failed to develop and accommodate the expanded participation—disorder and often violence followed. In the absence of institutionalized procedures and agreement on the legitimacy of such procedures, each group acted in politics in its own way and with its own weapons. The result was often a divided, praetorian society in which the "wealthy bribe; students riot; workers strike; mobs demonstrate; and the military coup."[15]

The transition from industrial to postindustrial society could conceivably pose comparable problems, although it will be difficult for the expansion of participation to be as extensive as it was in the earlier transition. Nonetheless the problem of broadened participation and stultified institutions could still present itself. The principal institutions of political participation in industrial society are political parties, interest groups, associations, and elections. To what extent will these institutions be adapted to the broadened scope of political participation in postindustrial society? The core participant institution, the political party, appears to be verging on a state of institutional and political decay. Throughout much of the country, party machines have collapsed completely or become pale shadows of their former selves: weak in finances, personnel, resources, and organization. Party identification has weakened: the proportion of citizens who identify themselves as "independent" has risen significantly. The most dramatic increase is, moreover, among the younger voters: in 1950, 28 percent of the 21-to-29-year-old group identified as "independent"; in 1971, 43 percent of this age group did.[16] In addition, party voting has declined precipitously: in 1950 about 80 percent of the voters cast straight party ballots; in 1970 about 50 percent of the voters did.[17] Throughout the Western world the advent of industrial society was accompanied by the development of parties and frequently by intense levels of partisanship. Unless there is a clear-cut reversal of current trends, however, parties do not appear to be the likely mechanisms for structuring the higher levels of participation which should characterize postindustrial society. In this event, either new organizational forms for participation will be developed or postindustrial politics will assume a praetorian cast similar to that of so many societies when they moved from the agrarian to the industrial phase.

New structures for participation could take a variety of forms, of which two perhaps deserve special mention here. Middle-class suburban political participation often takes place through various forms of civic and community-oriented organizations. It may also, of course, lead to new forms of political party organization, in which ideological and civic motivations play a major role. The efforts to win the presidential nomination of their party by Goldwater in 1964, McCarthy in 1968, and McGovern in 1972 were fundamentally similar and in large part reflected the new types of political tactics, organization, and style which may become characteristic of postindustrial politics. In some instances, as with the Republican organization in Nassau County, New York, it may be possible to recreate many of the characteristics of the old-style central city machine in a suburban environment. More generally, however, suburban postindustrial politics is more likely to manifest itself in the form of "issue organizations" concerned with particular causes and problems and which may well succeed one another in rather bewildering fashion, with the same "concerned" people organizing themselves one year to protest a war, the next year to promote clean air, and the following year to reform the high-school curriculum. This pattern of sustained participation in transitory organizations has the double effect of meeting the needs of the educated suburbanites to be involved and at the same time it insures that their involvement will have little lasting impact on the decision-making process.

In addition to community-oriented participation in suburbia, postindustrial society is also likely to see greater job-oriented participation in the bureaucracies where most of the postindustrial society's white-collar workers work. The expansion of participation has to be reconciled in some way with the expansion of bureaucracy. Conceivably, new types of decentralized decision-making, participatory management, and even "worker control" could be developed to meet this need. Much more likely, however, is the simple intensification of existing trends toward white-collar unionism. The middle-class employees of government, educational institutions, medical institutions, and various service industries, in all of which employment is rapidly expanding, are increasingly coming to see the advantages of unionism and collective bargaining in terms of the achievement of their own interests. Teachers unions, the American Association of University Professors, the American Foreign Service Association, to cite only a few examples, are redefining their role from that of an essentially apolitical professional association to that of a representative organization devoted not simply to promoting professional communication among the members of the group but also to the representation of the interests of the group before high-level management and in competition with other groups. In a largely white-collar bureaucratic society, the political process will in large part be fought out in the competition among white-collar groups within the framework of the bureaucracy.

The expansion of participation could make postindustrial society an extraordinarily difficult form of society to govern. Increases in education and in the resulting sense of political efficacy mean an increase in the knowledge of political and social problems and of the desire to do something about those problems. They do not necessarily mean any change in the processes of political and governmental decision-making which will increase the capacity of society to do anything about those problems. Effective governmental action could be more rather than less difficult in a society with a more highly-educated and participant population. American cities with more highly-educated populations, for instance, tend to have fewer innovations than cities with less-educated populations. One reason suggested for this seemingly anomalous situation is that widespread education tends to produce too much interest and participation and that this leads to political stalemate. Innovation is easier when substantial portions of the population are indifferent.[18] Thus a society which is highly educated and hence presumably highly innovative technologically could be highly conservative politically, in terms not of the values of the population but of the output of the system.

In any fundamental change in the nature of society, some social forces gain in social status, economic position, and numerical strength, absolutely and relatively, while others lose in status, position, and numbers, absolutely or relatively. As a result, the transition from one form of society to

106

another often involves three major lines of cleavage: between rising and declining social forces; between declining social forces; and between rising social forces. The transition from agrarian to industrial society saw the decline of the land-owning elite and peasantry and the rise of the urban bourgeoisie and industrial proletariat. This produced conflict of rural landowners versus peasants, of urban bourgeoisie and workers versus rural landowners and peasants, and of urban bourgeoisie versus industrial workers. The transition from industrial to postindustrial society involves a decline in the relative number and status of blue-collar workers and central-city dwellers and an increase in the numbers and status of white-collar workers and suburbanites. This transition could involve three lines of cleavage comparable to those which characterized the earlier movement into industrial society.

In the first instance, the declining social forces conflict with each other, as blue-collar labor struggles with central city dwellers, primarily black, over segregation, schools, jobs, and welfare. This cleavage was, of course, a central focus of American politics in the late 1960s and early 1970s. In this process, history doubles back on itself so far as the blacks are concerned. In terms of the transition from agrarian to industrial society, the blacks are a rising social force, their migration to the cities and improvement in socioeconomic status resembling simultaneous processes in less-developed countries in Latin America and Asia. At the same time, however, the social-governmental unit to which they are moving is becoming less important in American society as the rest of that society begins the transit from the the industrial to the postindustrial phase. The migration of farmers to the cities in the United States and other Western societies in the nineteenth century and the parallel contemporary migrations taking place in the Third World have been accompanied by the "the rise of the city," with the principal locus of power and initiative shifting from rural to urban society. The migration of the blacks into the cities of

107

twentieth-century America, however, is accompanied by "the decline of the city" and its loss, relatively and absolutely, of numbers and influence to the suburbs. On the one hand, this dual transition reduces social conflict by substituting city-suburb segregation for rural-urban segregation; on the other hand, however, the longer-term impact may be for one cleavage to reinforce another and to intensify the problems of the blacks who are better prepared for life in industrial than in postindustrial society. To be a rising social force in a declining sector of society could be a recipe for intense frustration.

A second line of cleavage finds city dwellers and blue-collar workers with parallel interests aligned against the expanding white-collar and suburban social forces. Insofar as numbers are important in politics, the power of the latter should be growing while that of the former declines, and American politics should be taking on more and more of the characteristics associated with the politics of well-educated, white-collar suburbanites. In fact, however, numbers are not the only thing that counts, even in democratic politics and perhaps particularly in American politics. If the historical analogy with the shift from agrarian to industrial society means anything, a decline in the relative numbers, status, and position of a group does not necessarily lead to a decline in political power. The less important the farmers became in American society, the more powerful they became in American government. Declining social forces, indeed, often are galvanized into political action precisely because they are declining. Threatened by the apparent flow of events, they are stimulated to greater unity, better organization, and more vigorous action to protect their interests, entrenching themselves behind political and legal barricades, using the power of the state to preserve a privileged position. In the United States, the declining farmers first gave birth to populism, which failed precisely because the farmers were no longer a popular majority, and then turned to organization and interest group politics, particularly through the Farm

Bureau Federation. As a result, the decrease in the number of farmers was accompanied by an increase in government benefits for farmers. Somewhat similarly, the decline of the "old middle class" of independent professional men, shop-keepers, small businessmen generated various right-wing movements in the United States and, in Europe, contributed to the rise of fascism.

In the transition from industrial to postindustrial society, the comparable declining groups are blue-collar workers and central-city dwellers. In the past, the political activities of these groups have, in large part, focused on electoral politics. The big city machines were, of course, primarily concerned with the control of their own local government, but they were also often major factors in state politics and in the outcome of presidential elections in the large industrial states. Similarly, the political activity of organized labor progressed from the Gompers efforts to reward friends and punish enemies through the CIO Political Action Committee to the more recent important political role of Committee on Political Education (COPE) both within the Democratic party and in supporting labor-endorsed Democratic candidates. The electoral power of the central cities and of union labor, symbolized dramatically in the aging personalities of Chicago Mayor Richard Daley and labor leader George Meany, is, however, clearly on the decline in comparison with that of other groups. Just as the farmers shifted from efforts to develop popular majorities, the political spokesmen for the central cities and blue-collar labor will more and more resort to interest group politics and to the effort to carve out semiautonomous arenas, governmental "whirlpools" as Ernest Griffiths once called them, within which they can play a dominant role and which will be protected by law, custom, and governmental organization from the impact of broader constituencies. They will thus maintain a toe-hold on the political system and a firm claim on resources distributed through the political system.

The efforts of the central cities and blue-collar labor to

109

defend their interests against a population which is increasingly suburban and white-collar could generate among those groups an increasing sense of group identity and class consciousness. In the European context, in which social classes are in general more sharply articulated, class consciousness is often most intense when a group has begun to develop economically and socially and then attempts to establish itself firmly in the political sphere. Limitations on individual mobility lead to group consciousness among the members of the excluded groups, with this group consciousness reaching its most intense form in the final stages of the efforts by the group to win acceptance as a part of the established social, economic, and political order. In the United States, on the other hand, upward mobility has been an individual as well as a group phenomenon. Subjectively and objectively, rising social forces have been relatively easily absorbed into the great amorphous American middle class. As a result, the integration of a group into society has not been accompanied by the same levels of group consciousness as it typically has in Europe. On the other hand, a perceived threat to a group which does occupy a well established and accepted position in the political, economic, social system is likely to generate higher levels of group consciousness. Groups become most conscious of their common identity and interests not when they are making their way up in American society but rather when they are on the verge of being forced down. Consequently, the emergence of a postindustrial society is likely to increase the class consciousness and cohesion of blue-collar workers and also of central-city dwellers. In addition, for many cities, of course, a majority of the population will belong to racial minorities. The "central city consciousness" which emerges as a result of the relative decline of the central city in social importance is likely to be reinforced by racial consciousness, which is the one area of American society where the European pattern of "consciousness when on the rise" tends to prevail, precisely because, of course, the barriers against the individual mobility of blacks have

110

been comparable to those in Europe against the individual mobility of workers.

A third line of cleavage (comparable to that between capitalists and workers in industrial society) could be between those white-collar workers in the public sector and those in the private sector. The former will want increasing wages and other economic benefits; the latter will not want to pay for these through higher taxes. The interaction between owners and workers in the private sector of industrial society could be reenacted in the interaction between white-collar bureaucrats and white-collar taxpayers in post-industrial society.

This conflict will place enormous strains on political leadership at all levels of government. Through unionization and threats of disruption in essential services, public-sector employees can pressure, induce, or coerce political leaders to meet their demands. The trend toward white-collar unionism is perhaps strongest among governmental employees. In 1971, 52 percent of the civilians working for the federal government were either union members or members of quasi-union associations. Indicative of the trend, in the fall of 1972, the American Foreign Service Association, previously a standard type of professional organization, won an election to become the bargaining agent for the foreign service officers of both the State Department and the Agency for International Development, (AID). Increasing unionization led to more strikes. In 1961, there were only 28 strikes reported involving governmental employees; in 1966, there were 142 such strikes; in 1970 there were 412. The benefits of unionization, however, are real: the salaries of unionized teachers, for instance, average 4 to 15 percent more than those of nonunionized teachers in comparable jobs.[19]

Political leaders will also be subject to strong electoral pressure, if they wish to continue in office, to avoid any increase in taxes. The easy escape—indeed, perhaps the only escape—from this dilemma is to increase wages without increasing taxes which presumably will mean high and prob-

111

ably increasing rates of inflation. Apart from this out, it is not clear that any industrial or postindustrial society has resolved the problem of how to reconcile the freedom of public employees to organize and to strike, on the one hand, with the selection of public officials through competitive elections, on the other.

The difficulty of keeping white-collar, public-sector wages under control will be all the greater because of the absence of any clear criterion by which to judge when such wage increases are justified. In most industrial work, wages can be tied to, or at least debated in terms of, increases in productivity. In a postindustrial society, however, the concept of "productivity" is of dubious relevance. In the first place, the transition from industrial to postindustrial society is marked precisely by the decline of those industries in which productivity increases (as usually measured) are highest and the growth of those sectors of the economy in which productivity increases are lowest. The concept of "productivity," in a sense, may be one which is peculiarly appropriate only to industrial society. Secondly, even if the concept is relevant in postindustrial society, the problem of measuring it becomes increasingly difficult. The concept is useful enough when applied to a factory assembly line of blue-collar workers; it is generally difficult to apply to a bureaucratic office manned by white-collar workers, and it is particularly difficult to apply to many service industries. As Peter Drucker has observed, "We have yet to learn what productivity really means" in nonmanual work. "Yet the sales clerk and the college teacher, the nurse and the marketing manager, the policeman and the accountant all expect their incomes to rise as fast as that of the manual worker."[20] In the absence of even a relatively "objective" standard such as productivity by which to evaluate wage claims, the competition between bureaucrats who want more and political leaders who want reelection is likely to be determined not by any appeal to reason but primarily by the application of political muscle.

Societies are divided not only socially but institutionally. Historically most societies have one or more central institutional cleavages cutting across their political system. In traditional agrarian societies, the central institutional cleavage was often between the monarchy and bureaucracy in the centralized bureaucratic empires, between church and state in medieval feudalism, and then between absolute monarchy and parliament with the rise of the middle class. In Western industrial society, institutional cleavage was itself institutionalized in the competition between political parties. In the United States, this unplanned development was added to a constitutional system which was consciously designed to pit three branches and two levels of government against each other. During its industrial phase, American political history has in large part been written in terms of the changing balances of power between the two parties, between state government and national government, and between executive and legislature. In one form or another, these conflicts will undoubtedly continue. Recent trends, however, suggest an attenuation of party conflict, the dominance of the national government vis-a-vis the states, and the growing strength of the executive in relation to Congress. At times there may be brief slowdowns or reversals in these trends such as the efforts by Congress to reassert its role in the legislative process and its control over foreign policy in the late 1960s and early 1970s. The longer-term secular trends are, however, clearly in the other direction. Undoubtedly in the future party conflict, legislative-executive conflict, and state-national conflict will remain significant features of the American political scene, but they seem less likely to play as central a role in postindustrial as they did in industrial society.

The decline in the critical importance of these cleavages, however, may well be matched by the rise in importance of a new institutional cleavage between the executive bureaucracy and mass media. The size, impact, and influence of each of these institutions is clearly growing. Their interests clearly differ. The projection of current trends would thus suggest that this cleavage would play a critical role in future politics. Deduction from the prevailing model of postindustrial society leads to a similar conclusion. Postindustrial society is highly bureaucratized with the public bureaucracy clearly playing a central role in the allocation of costs and benefits. The developments in electronic communication, on the other hand, give the mass media, particularly television, a central role in shaping public attitudes and the political process. The more familiar forms of political organization such as parties and legislatures are thus pressed by the development of executive bureaucracy, on the one hand, and the emergence of the mass media, on the other.

A three-way power struggle is likely to dominate postindustrial politics in the United States. The top politcal leaders of the country, the president and his White House associates, are, on the one hand, faced with the need to use the media to generate political support for themselves and their policies and to use the bureaucracy in order to carry out their policies. On the other hand, they are also confronted with the need to counterbalance both bureaucracy and media, each of which can and does act in its own interests in ways counter to those of the president and the presidency. At times bureaucrats and media will act together against the political leadership; at other times president and bureaucrats will act against the media; and, perhaps less frequently (since the interests of the media naturally align themselves with political leaders out of power), the president and media will confront the bureaucrats. In postindustrial society, power goes to those political leaders who have access to the media and who command compliance from the bureaucracy. The ability to achieve the former will in large part determine who gets into office; the ability to achieve the latter will in large part determine what he can do once he gets there.

Political leaders and the press have historically complained about the treatment they receive from each other. In the 1960s, however, the issues between government and

114

press began to take on more of an institutional character. Increasingly the press came to define itself as more explicitly political. A dominant trend within the media was the redefinition of their role from that of a relatively detached reporter of events to that of an engagee shaper of events. The norms of advocatory journalism challenged those of objective journalism. In large part, this was a natural result of the growing influence of both the media and the governmental bureaucracy. "The national media," as Theodore H. White observed, "have put themselves into the role of permanent critical opposition to any government which does not instantly clean up the unfinished business of our time." Hence "no government will satisfy them."[21] The national media—that is, primarily the National Broadcasting Company, the Columbia Broadcasting System, and the American Broadcasting Company, the *New York Times,* the *Washington Post*—increasingly came to conceive of themselves in an adversary role vis-a-vis the executive government. At stake were not just conflicting personalities and differing political viewpoints, but also fairly fundamental institutional interests. The media have an interest in exposure, criticism, highlighting and encouraging disagreement and disaffection within the executive branch. The leaders of the executive branch have an interest in secrecy, hierarchy, discipline, and the suppression of criticism. The function of the press is to expand political debate and involvement; the natural instinct of the bureaucracy is to limit it.

The types of conflicts between the government and media which came to the fore in the early 1970s are likely to reappear in the future. In the most notable confrontation between media and executive, the Pentagon Papers case, the press won a major battle against prior restraint. (In an almost simultaneous happening, the press also scored an important victory when the House of Representatives refused 226 to 181 to vote a contempt citation against CBS requested by one of its members. To secure this outcome, CBS reportedly mobilized its several hundred local affiliates across the country to bring pressure on their congressmen.) In other instances involving the right of reporters to refuse to disclose sources of information before grand juries, the press initially won in the lower courts but then, in the Caldwell Case, lost before the Nixon Supreme Court. In the following year a number of reporters were either jailed briefly or threatened with jail for failing to respond to questions from prosecutors in grand jury hearings.

The role of the media in the 1970s paralleled rather strikingly that of another rising social force, the industrial corporations, in the 1880s and 1890s. In that period of transition from agrarian to industrial society, the developing business groups expounded a laissez-faire philosophy, condemning governmental control of business and even criticizing efforts to develop self-regulation by business. Similar stands are now taken by the press against the government and public control. Like business the press identifies the public interest with its interest and elaborates novel constitutional interpretations to forward that interest. In the late nineteenth century, business groups rallied around the "right to property"; in the late twentieth century the press rallies about the "right to know." The rising business groups, in the earlier transition, seized upon the due process of law clause of the Fourteenth Amendment to defend themselves against government controls; in the transition to postindustrial society, the media attempt to make comparable use of the freedom of the press clause of the First Amendment. In due course, business was checked by the countervailing power of government and other social forces; in due course, the media will probably suffer a similar fate.

The change from traditional to modern society was nowhere more dramatic than in the area of political beliefs and ideologies. Among the later developing countries in particular, this contrast was all the more stark since modern values were in large part foreign values, brought into the society from abroad either by colonial rulers or by groups from the traditional society such as students and military officers who

116

had been exposed abroad to such values. The latter often returned home filled with contempt for the "backwardness" of their own society and resentment against the ruling groups which could be held responsible for that backwardness. They hence attempted to overthrow the traditional order, to centralize power in themselves, and to introduce far-reaching modernizing reforms to make their country respectable in their own eyes and in those of the world. The result was a sharp cleavage in political goals and values between the modern and traditional groups and, often, also, among modernizing groups (bourgeoisie vs. military vs. intellectuals) who assigned different priorities to different modernizing values (economic development vs. administrative efficiency vs. egalitarian nationalism). Not infrequently, the assertion of modern ideologies also gave rise to the reassertion and at times creation of traditional or traditionalizing counterideologies. The new ideologies, of course, generally were introduced by the offspring of the upper ruling classes, who used them to challenge the authority of their elders and of the conservative institutions in their society. The latter, in turn, used religious values to mobilize the masses against the modernizers.

The ideological cleavage was substantially less among the early modernizers, but it still existed. Comparable patterns could well characterize the shift from industrial to postindustrial society. The political values prevalent in post-industrial society are likely to be significantly different from those dominant in industrialism. Many years ago David Riesman suggested some of these differences in his analysis of inner-directed and other-directed character types. In the early 1970s, Ronald Inglehart pointed to a somewhat parallel change in fundamental value priorities as a result of increasing affluence and education. His data show that younger, more affluent Europeans give greater weight to "needs for belonging and intellectual and esthetic self-fulfillment" (which he calls postbourgeois values) than do older and poorer people, who give first priority to material and economic values.[22] He argues, reasonably persuasively, that this shift is a generational change rather than a life-cycle phenomenon: that (see Rostow, Mann, and the "Buddenbrooks dynamics" argument) what was important for one generation to achieve is of secondary importance to the next generation because it already has it. As a result of these changes, the middle class becomes radical and the working class conservative, but the overall movement of society is in a left direction.

Those value differences between generations and classes provide a basis for ideological cleavage. Ideology flourishes in periods of rapid and destabilizing change. If the transition to postindustrial society is of any duration, ideological formulations reflecting the interests of rising and declining social forces are likely to surface from time to time. In addition, a more highly-educated citizenry may in some sense *require* ideology to become mobilized in politics.

The role of ideology in the shift to postindustrialism would appear, nonetheless, to be rather different from its role in the transition to industrial society. In the earlier transition, ideology seemed to play an independent role in furnishing the purposes and framework for social and political action. The rise of the bourgeoisie and the emergence of industrial society in the West would have been quite different without the "Protestant ethic." Without Marxist-Communist ideology, the histories of the countries which adopted the Communist variant of industrialization and industrial society also would have been fundamentally different. In this sense, ideology—liberal, Communist, Socialist—played a major role in shaping the form, timing, and substance of industrial society.

Postindustrial society, however, at least as it is emerging in the United States, does not seem to be a product of any set of "postindustrial ideologies." It is rather the consequence of ongoing social and economic processes which have developed during the last years of industrial society and of a period which was held to epitomize "the end of ideology."

Postindustrial society has theorists but not ideologists: or at least the postindustrial Marx seems yet to make his appearance on the world stage. In fact, while one can think of industrial society being at least in part a product of industrializing ideologies, the reverse would seem to be true with respect to postindustrialism. Those ideas and values which have been labeled "postindustrial" or "postbourgeois" appear to be the product of the trends toward postindustrial society and, in some measure, a reaction against those trends. It might be possible to interpret postbourgeois values, middle-class radicalism, the counterculture, and the general mental outlook which seems so prominent in Sweden and in certain circles in the United States as a romantic, Luddite reaction against the bureaucratic and technological tendencies of postindustrialism. Yet the problem here is that these values and attitudes are strongest precisely among those groups which postindustrial society is making more numerous and more important. They are more prevalent among the young, the college-educated, and the affluent. They are less prevalent among those groups declining in importance on the postindustrial scene.

Postindustrial society may thus give rise to social and political beliefs and attitudes which challenge many of the institutions of that society. At the extreme, this may lead to some younger elements of the strata spawned by postindustrial society to withdraw from that society, their places presumably being taken by the offspring of lower-class, working-class, and lower-middle-class groups which have not yet been absorbed into the postindustrial milieu. Or, to adopt the colorful language of the Bergers, the greening of the youth may lead to the blueing of the Establishment.[23]

The conflict between ideology and institutions is a recurring one in American history. The prevailing ideas of the American creed have been those of liberalism, individualism, equality, constitutionalism, rights against the state. They have been against hierarchy, discipline, government, organization, and specialization. The major periods of

119

fundamental change in American history have been those when social forces have emerged which reinvigorated the creed and hence stimulated new attacks on established authority. This confrontation occurred during the Jacksonian period with the attack on the undemocratic elements of the constitutional system, at the time of the Civil War with the opposition to slavery extension and to the slave system in the southern states, and in the 1890s with the Populist and Progressive response to the rise of industrial corporations. The confrontation between ideology and institutions in postindustrial society thus fits into a well-established American pattern. The ideology of postindustrialism is, indeed, in large part a redefinition of the traditional ideas of the American creed in the context of this new type of society. Insofar, however, as the postindustrial society is more highly educated and more participant than American society has been in the past and insofar as American political institutions will be more bureaucratic and hierarchical than they have been in the past, the conflict between ideology and institutions could be more intense than it has been in the past.

Comparable questions may arise about the implications of postindustrial values for the security of the nation-state. The values which are alleged to prevail in postindustrial society could weaken the military security of such societies. If the predictions are accurate, strong opposition will exist to military service and to taxation for military purposes. Many of these antimilitary trends can now clearly be seen in Western Europe and the United States. At the same time, sustained military research and development produces greater emphasis on sophisticated weapons. The logic of these trends points in the direction of a small, highly technical, professionalized military force. This could put postindustrial societies at the military mercy of other societies which are able to mobilize and equip substantial conventional forces. To what extent would a postindustrial society be capable of pursuing foreign policy goals which required the use of military force for purposes other than simply its own survival? To what extent would a postindustrial society be able and willing even to defend its own independent existence?

Deductions from the socioeconomic model of postindustrial society plus projections of current trends in the United States suggest, on first glance, an overall movement toward a more rationalized, bureaucratic pattern of politics in which basic cleavages over who gets what are muted or sublimated and in which politics and political conflict, particularly class conflict as it has been known in the past, do not occupy the center of the stage. The analogy with the agrarian-to-industrial transition, however, would suggest a very different pattern: one of increasing socioeconomic dislocation, frustrated expectations, intensifying conflicts, disorder, and violence. A more extensive, even if still rather limited, exploration of postindustrial politics in terms of projections and deductions such as has been attempted here indicates that the implications from analogy may well have a deeper relevance. The struggles among rising and declining social forces, the institutional conflict between governmental bureaucracy and mass media, the higher levels of political participation, the prevalence of oppositional political values and ideologies among key elements of the population, and particularly the fundamental conflict between the demands which are made on government—particularly by its own employees—and the resources which citizens are willing to make available to government, all forecast a high level of political tension and strife.

If postindustrial society emerges along the lines its theorists expect and if it has the political consequences which we have suggested here, the prevailing forms of government and decision-making in the United States will be put to some crucial tests. The ways of recruiting political leaders and the skills of political leaders are not likely to change substantially. Higher levels of intelligence and knowledge do not necessarily translate into more skillful political judgments and decisions. Recent history in the United States has demonstrated conclusively that the brightest and the best in

121

universities and in suburbs are often eager victims of political hysteria and demagoguery. In postindustrial society, the media will furnish the new opportunities for the mobilization of mass movements by political leaders. At the same time, the executive bureaucracy will increasingly impinge on the lives of the citizens. These tendencies may be countered by new forms and structures of political participation. The question remains how the central institutions of government, which still bear the imprint of the eighteenth century, will be able to function in this environment.

The tensions which are likely to prevail in a postindustrial society are likely to require a more authoritiative and effective pattern of governmental decision-making. The trends in terms of values, ideology, and participation, however, may make the authoritative allocation of resources by government more rather than less difficult. Every form of society—even a family —needs a certain measure of deference, authority, and hierarchy if it is to function well. A postindustrial society will need these at least as much and perhaps more than its predecessors. Yet these are precisely the concepts which seem to be at odds with the values generated by the social-economic advances of postindustrial society. Social cohesiveness and institutional adaptivity will clearly be put under pressure. The issue for postindustrial society is to what extent the social consequences of achieving postindustrialism are compatible with the political requisites for maintaining society. All in all, postindustrial politics is likely to be the darker side of postindustrial society and measurably less benign than industrial politics.

The saving grace, however, could be that postindustrial society may not emerge in the same way and to the same extent that it has been thought that it would. Models of the social-economic characteristics of postindustrial society are, in large part, a product of the projection of trends prevalent in the United States and other highly developed countries in the 1950s and 1960s. Conceivably, these trends could level off or even reverse themselves. In the United States, for instance, the expansion of college enrollments has already dropped off; in 1972 less than 58 percent of the white males in the the 18-19 age group were enrolled in college as compared with 44 percent three years earlier. The proportion of the GNP devoted to research and development has also decreased from its high in the mid-1960s.[24] The movement to suburbia continues but at what appears to be a slackened pace, and in some cases central cities are resuming their population growth. In general, moreover, models of future societies which grip the imagination and seem overwhelmingly persuasive and definitive intellectually, also seldom materialize in practice. In part this is because any model abstracts from reality, and historical reality in turn retaliates by evolving in ways not contemplated in the model. In part, also, the process of setting forth a model of the future in itself may stimulate countercurrents which limit the likelihood of its being realized. In addition, a model of a future society normally focuses on what is different from existing society and, in some measure, implies a break with that society. In fact, however, the slate is rarely if ever wiped clean. A model of a new society, consequently, is only a partial model of future society. What is new more often supplements rather than supplants what is old.

Social science analysis of the transition from agrarian to industrial society began with a clear-cut dichotomy between what was modern and what was traditional. It soon became clear, however, that the process of modernization did not involve the displacement of the latter by the former, but rather the addition of modern elements to an ongoing society which still retained many of its traditional components. In many cases indeed, traditional values, behavior patterns, forms of organization were reinvigorated and strengthened by the process which was initially supposed to destroy them.[25] Just as this earlier transition produced neo-traditionalism, so also the current transition may lead to neoindustrialism. The society of the future, in any event, will be a mixture of industrial and postindustrial components. If

123

this mixture is heavily weighted in the postindustrial direction, its politics will also be both different and unpleasant. But if postindustrial society is, in fact, not all that different from industrial society, its political traumas and conflicts will be less intense and more familiar.

Notes

1. Bell discusses the distant and immediate antecedents of the postindustrial society concept in the "The Post-Industrial Society: The Evolution of an Idea," *Survey*, 17 (Spring 1971): 102-68. Zbigniew Brzezinski has made a good case for labeling this phenomenon "technetronic society," *Between Two Ages: America's Role in the Technetronic Era* (New York: Viking Press, 1970), p.9. But Bell's name seems to have caught on.

2. See Daniel Bell, "The Measurement of Knowledge and Technology," in Eleanor Sheldon and Wilbert Moore, eds., *Indicators of Social Change* (New York: Russell Sage, 1968), pp. 152-58; Brzezinski, *Between Two Ages,* pp. 10-14; Herman Kahn and Anthony J. Wiener, *The Year 2000* (New York: Macmillan, 1967), p.186. Kahn and Wiener also appear uncertain about their uncertainty on the erosion of national interest values. On p. 25 of the same book the same list appears without the question mark after this item.

3. Bell, *Survey,* 17 (Spring 1971), 165; "Technocracy and Politics," Ibid., 16 (Winter 1971), 1, 4, 9-10, 19; in Sheldon and Moore, *Indicators,* p. 158; "Notes on the Post-Industrial Society (II)," *Public Interest,* no. 7 (Spring 1967): 108-10.

4. Brzezinski, *Between Two Ages,* pp. 11-13, 108, 219.

5. Christopher Lasch, "Toward a Theory of Post-Industrial Society," in M. Donald Hancock and Gideon Sjoberg, eds., *Politics in the Post-Welfare State* (New York: Columbia University Press, 1972), pp. 44-48.

6. Bell, *Survey,* 17 (Spring 1971): 164.

7. Karl W. Deutsch, "Social Mobilization and Political Development," *American Political Science Review,* 55 (September 1961): 493-514.

8. Bell, *Survey,* 16 (Winter 1971): 6; Lasch, in Hancock and Sjoberg, *Post-Welfare State,* p. 36.

9. Constance Serrentino, "Comparing Employment Shifts in 10 Industrialized Countries," *Monthly Labor Review,* 94 (October 1971): 6.

10. See figures in table from census and compare Bell, in Sheldon and Moore, *Indicators,* pp. 204-205, 217.

11. See "Organisation for Economic Co-operation and Development," *Reviews of National Science Policy: United States (Paris: OECD, 1968), p. 30.*

12. *U. S. Bureau of the Census, Statistical Abstract of the United States: 1970* (Washington, 91st ed., 1970), p. 368; Ibid.: 1972, 93rd ed., p. 374. The total turnout figure is the *actual* turnout; the figures for the turnout of different educational classes are *reported* turnout by survey. The total reported turnout is 67.8 percent; 6 percent of the population, in short, say they voted when they did not.

13. See Sidney Verba and Norman H. Nie, *Participation in America: Political Democracy and Social Equality* (New York: Harper & Row, 1972), p. 100.

14. Louis Harris, "What the Nixon Landslide Means," *Chicago Tribune,* no. 18, 1972, p. 12.

15. Samuel P. Huntington, *Political Order in Changing Societies* (New Haven: Yale University Press, 1968), p. 196.

16. Gallup Survey, reported in *New York Times,* October 17, 1971, p. 34.

17. Frederick G. Dutton, *Changing Sources of Power: American Politics in the 1970s* (New York: McGraw-Hill, 1971), p. 228. See generally Walter DeVries and V. Lance Tarrance, *The Ticket-Splitter: A New Force in American Politics* (Grand Rapids: William B. Eerdmans, 1972).

18. Robert L. Crain and Donald B. Rosenthal, "Communty Status as a Dimension of Local Decision-Making," *American Sociological Review* 32 (December 1967): 970-84. See Robert R. Alford and Eugene C. Lee, "Voting Turnout in American Cities," *American Political Science Review* 62 (September 1968): 796-813, who found lower voting turnouts in more highly educated cities, but who hypothesized that more educated people may rely on other forms of political participation.

19. Tax Foundation, Inc., *Unions and Government Employment* (New York: Tax Foundation, Inc., 1972), pp. 29, 39-41. See also Harry H. Wellington and Ralph K. Winter, Jr., *The Unions and the Cities* (Washington, D.C.: Brookings Institution, 1971); David T. Stanley, *Managing Local Government Under Pressure* (Washington: Brookings Institution, 1972); Charles L. Schultze, Edward R. Fried, Alice M. Rivlin, Nancy H. Teeters, *Setting National Priorities: The 1973 Budget* (Washington: Brookings Institution, 1972), pp. 296-301; Sam Zagoria, ed., *Public Workers and Public Unions* (Englewood Cliffs, N.J.: Prentice-Hall, 1972).

20. Peter F. Drucker, "The Surprising Seventies," *Harper's,* 243 (July 1971): 39.

21. Theodore H. White, "America's Two Cultures," *Columbia Journalism Review,* Winter 1969-70, p. 8, quoted in Robert L. Bartley, "The Press: Adversary, Surrogate Sovereign, or Both?" (Paper presented at Annual Meeting, American Political Science Association, Chicago, Ill., September 7-11, 1971), p. 3. See also Daniel P. Moynihan's perceptive discussion, "The Presidency and the Press," *Commentary,* 51 (March 1971): 41-52.

22. Ronald Inglehart, "The Silent Revolution in Europe: Intergenerational Change in Post-Industrial Societies," *American Political Science Review* 65 (December 1971): 991-1017.

23. Peter L. and Brigitte Berger, "The Blueing of

America," *New Republic* 164 (April 3, 1971): 20-23.

24. U. S. Bureau of the Census, *School Enrollment in the United States: 1972 (Advance Data)* (Washington, D. C., Series P-20, no. 247, 1973), reported by Jack Rosenthal, *New York Times,* February 25, 1973; National Science Foundation, *Research and Development in Industry 1970* (Washington, D.C. NSF 72-309, 1972), p. 3.

25. See my discussion of "modernization revisionism," "The Change to Change: Modernization, Development, and Politics," *Comparative Politics* 3 (April 1971): 293 ff.

Part IV
The City

Chapter Six

Information, the Postindustrial Society, and the American City

Nathan Glazer

To speak of the city in the context of the informational revolution is to conjure up rosy visions of the future—a future in which the choice of different informational means and mechanisms is infinitely expanded, and in which presumably the satisfactions and pleasures to be derived from an expansion of knowledge for its own sake, or for a better understanding of one's place in the world, or as a means of improving one's own happiness and effectiveness, continually grow. It is to think of a society in which the telephone is expanded and supplemented with the picturephone, in which the few channels of existent television are expanded with the many choices of cable television, in which the waits for public transportation and the inconvenience of using one's own car are replaced by a personally summoned general transit vehicle operated by computer, in which waits at hospitals and for medical examinations are reduced or eliminated by a highly efficient system of transportation, in which the system of education that now concentrates with inadequate effectiveness on children, adolescents and youths, is expanded to cover preschool children and postschool adults, providing a rich diet of relevant information in settings which will make the present school appear as outdated as the early coal mine with its child and women employees appears to us now. Inevitably, in other words, it is to present an optimistic perspective, even if one which undoubtedly introduces certain more somber complexities—the dangers of sabotage in an increasingly sophisticated and sensitive system of communication, the problem of information and communication overload, the problem of individual privacy in an age in which picturephones stand in every home, and the like.

But whereas such an optimistic perspective may be reasonable for the Japanese city, it seems scarcely relevant to the problems of the American city. What are the problems of the American city, as seen by its inhabitants? I will list a few, in the rough order of felt discomfort, and suggest which ones may be amenable to improvement through information, present or future.

1. Crime and personal safety
2. Heavy individual taxes, particularly on property
3. Conflicts over race; principally over the integration of black children with white children in schools; more moderately over the movement of blacks into white areas; generally, over the representation of blacks in city services such as police and fire and sanitation departments, in particular those that have had strong linkages with other ethnic groups, and for which the route of entry does not involve a high level of education, and in which the returns in terms of salary and fringe benefits are, for the level of education represented, substantial
4. Expensive housing

5. Inadequate city services in various areas—speaking in New York, we can report one of these as sanitation
6. Issues of congestion in transportation
7. Environmental issues as such—smog, dirt, noise

Other problems can be listed, and there are various ways of presenting more basic issues as factors of some order of significance in these visible and immediately felt problems. Thus the enormous increase in the proportion of city populations now made up of blacks has in various ways contributed to and exacerbated these problems. Twenty-one percent of the population of central cities of metropolitan areas are now black and 28 percent of the population in the central cities of the largest metropolitan areas, those with populations of more than two million, are black. One might well view the problems of crime, heavy property taxes, and inadequate city services as in some way resultant from this radical and relatively recent population change. Of course there is a substantial and growing black middle class. But blacks—and Puerto Ricans in the Northeast, and Mexican-Americans in the Southwest—contribute disproportionately to the poor population. Inevitably a poor and deprived population, and one coming from rural areas and small towns into larger cities, will make some disproportionate contribution to crime and require some disproportionate share of city services. Perhaps the only aspect of urban discomfort which cannot be ascribed in large measure to the heavy increase in black populations is that stemming from items 6 and 7 on our list: the discomfort of commuting to and from jobs, by whatever means; and the environmental issues; for these are found in all great cities, regardless of racial composition and racial conflicts. And undoubtedly the poor and the black contribute *less* to congestion and physical environmental decline than the affluent and the white.

Another way of finding some basic factor which contributes to all these elements of felt discomfort is in the political and fiscal relationships between American cities and the

133

states and federal government, a relationship which I believe is unique among the developed nations of the world. The key problem in these relationships is the confinement of the political and fiscal authority of the central cities to a relatively limited part, geographically speaking, of their metropolitan areas. This means that the major costs of those city services that rise with rising proportions of black and poor—welfare, health, policing, fire protection, and so forth—must be borne by the central city. The central city is also restricted in its tax base. While it may have the major commercial property and office properties, industrial plants increasingly migrate outside the city where there is more and cheaper land, and less congestion. Retail stores follow the more prosperous part of the population to the suburbs. And even offices now migrate to the suburbs, where they have access to a better labor force, reduced costs of commutation, and less crime and dirt than in the city. Finally, the central city is in disproportionate measure the seat of nontaxpaying hospitals, universities and colleges, churches, and federal offices. Thus increasing costs combine with a decreasing tax base to create fiscal crises for the city. These we understand from current analyses will be less severe in the 1970s than they were in the 1960s, because the drop in the birth rate will reduce the pressure on schools and the costs of crime, and because federal revenue sharing is finally distributing some of the large sums raised through the federal income tax directly to the city.

But whatever the immediate prospects for the fiscal crisis, the fiscal and political relationships of American cities with higher levels of government are unique. While the federal government may ease the financial crisis of the central city, the central city remains limited to a poorer share of the metropolitan area and hemmed in by independent cities and towns. It can do nothing to change its boundaries and to expand the geographical scope of city government so that it may benefit from the presence of more prosperous suburban taxpayers, private and business, and may benefit from a

134

reduced burden of the poor. Nor, despite their formal constitutional powers, will the states intervene. As against the pattern of England and Japan, where city boundaries may be altered by a central government for the achievement of greater efficiency in the provision of services, here we are dependent on efforts at annexation requiring the consent of all parties—efforts which generally fail—or to ad hoc and independent agencies set up as alliances of cities and towns or as creatures independent of them which take up the task of achieving some level of efficiency in at least those areas where some sort of metropolitan-wide authority is essential—transportation, in particular.

But now let us return to the theme of information. Whether we consider the felt discomforts, or the two possible underlying causes for these discomforts I have discussed, it is hard to see what the contribution of information can be. We are in a situation where those discomforts that come relatively far down on the list can most obviously be in some way helped by advances in information. Certainly we can hope that the physical environment of the city may be so improved. We can hope that transportation congestion may be improved. When we come to inadequate city services we must have more modest hopes. While the problem of cleaning the city and protecting it from fire may be seen as purely technological and improvable by new technological means, there is a considerable social component involved in these services, and for them improvements in information or technology may not help.

For example, the Rand Corporation has for some years conducted studies of various New York City departments in order to improve city services. The Rand Corporation's greatest strength is in its combination of the technically proficient with social scientists. It has had to deal with the difficult problem of suspicion against all outsiders that dominates such enormous departments in New York as that of police, sanitation, and fire—a suspicion which is well documented in Wallace Sayre's and Herbert Kaufman's

135

classic *Governing New York City*. The Rand people have been most successful in developing good relations with the fire department, in part because their technological expertise came up with early proposals that were usable, and heightened the department's effectiveness in fighting fires in ways which did not challenge any institutional arrangement or interest. Thus Rand proposed the addition of a chemical to water which made it more slippery and permitted a greater volume of water to be directed on a fire with the same equipment. However, when it proposed to the sanitation department a more efficient deployment of men and trucks so that they could be used at the times and in the areas where collections were most needed, it inevitably met the resistance of the union, which preferred the old arrangements. In slum areas it is the weekends that produce the greatest amount of street garbage, but the sanitation department's men, protected by their union, fought the changes in deployment responsive to these facts. Information, which had determined a better system of deployment, was limited in overcoming entrenched interests.

A similar analysis was carried through for the police force and demonstrated that the police could be far more efficient in carrying out their functions of fighting crime if they were redeployed in accordance with the rates of crimes in different neighborhoods at different times. Here the difficulties of responding to better information were even greater. The New York City police must, according to state law, work according to a number of fixed schedules with the same number of police in each schedule. The power of the Policemen's Benevolent Association, extended to the state legislature, guarantees that the deployment the police find most convenient and popular—and one which ensures that relatively few of them will be around to fight crime when it is most rampant—is written into state law and immune to change by a conscientious police chief guided by the scientific analyses of the New York City Rand Institute.

I do not want to paint the picture in too deep a black: after one knows that one or another deployment of sanitation workers or policemen is more efficient than the patterns frozen into union contracts and state laws, changes *are* possible, I believe some are taking place. Thus information and better technology of information processing, gathering, and analysis play a role, but only after a time and after considerable effort engaged in overcoming vested interests that will be generally quite resistant to any change, and often strong enough to resist it. I have spoken about policemen and firemen and sanitation workers, but of course whatever I say is equally true of social workers as well as teachers, whose union is one of the most powerful in New York.

But this is only the first level at which information may be left helpless. It was discovered by a simple statistical analysis that fires and false alarms together were a perfect index to the social characteristics of city areas. Fires and false alarms rose as a city area was poorer and blacker. Fires in effect were only another index to resentment, anger, poverty, discrimination. And what could information do about that? Something no doubt, but not very much.

For as we move up the scale of urban problems, the contribution of information becomes more and more modest: this is true of racial conflict, taxes, and crime. There is some potential contribution, no doubt, but the social roots of these problems are so complex that the solutions must be in the realm of politics: of new social policy, of the compromising of interests, of new forms of government for the city perhaps which express new kinds of interest. In the United States, as in some developing countries, racial and group harmony should probably be a greater and more significant objective than economic growth and new technology. Certainly many opinionmakers feel this way. Conceivably, as Amitai Etzioni has argued, we may circumvent the difficulties in the way of social and political solutions to social and political problems by technical solutions. Technical solutions may not need the mobilization of large areas of public opinion, the reconciling in public of diverse outlooks and interests, new legislation and new branches of administration. Many can be introduced quite simply, just as slippery water was introduced in the hoses of the fire department of New York. And, one may argue, if the fire department does a better job in fighting fires in the slums because of a technical improvement, then it will make some contribution, no matter how modest, to reducing the anger and resentment in the slums and thus introduce a larger measure of civil peace to affect those problems which seem immune to direct technical solution. There is something to this argument. And yet, one wonders whether the contribution will not be so miniscule as to be invisible. The fact is that the firemen who come into the slums to respond to fires with slippery water will be met with the same antagonism, the same rocks and missiles, that meet firemen who come to put out fires with regular water. And the missiles are thrown not because firemen are not good at putting out fires or are particularly brutal to the property of blacks and Puerto Ricans when they put out fires. They are attacked because they are overwhelmingly white and because they are seen as representing a distant and antagnostic government.

Similarly, information and advanced technology can do something for crime, of course. A buzzer in every apartment, television sets screening those who enter, better locks, more rapid response by police, and so on. And yet one is impressed by the simple social reality that crime has social roots, and technical improvements really do appear to shift it, rather than eliminate it. We have been engaged in our cities in a regular process of hardening one target after another against attack. When taxi drivers are killed, we put in screens to protect them from their passengers, or we require them to carry only change for $5. When the assault shifts to bus drivers, we harden that target—cashboxes that are unbreakable and to which only the home garage has access. We have hardened the all-night gas stations—or eliminated them. It is no surprise to those of us who wait to see what will be the next soft target to which crime is di-

138

verted to find that it has been that most unlikely setting of all—the public school—where teachers are now threatened and robbed in front of their students. (The *New York Times* of October 29, 1972, reports the discovery of a new and even more ingenious "soft target": the philanthropic businessmen who go to churches to distribute free breakfasts to poor children. Two had just been robbed in a church.)

I have suggested that the problems that afflict great American cities are so ordered that those that may be attacked through the new information and the new technology of a postindustrial society tend to be those that are not at the top of the citizens' priority list. Japan and the United States may together attack the problems of urban pollution and transportation congestion and inadequate housing, but while these *are* the most severely felt of Japanese city problems, I do not believe they are the most severely felt of American city problems. These—crime, taxes, and racial conflict—are inextricably tied up with questions of race, even though race is only part of the explanation of high crime, high taxes, and even racial social conflict. However, even those problems that seem best suited to solution through technical means involve, in the United States, social and racial considerations. Perhaps in Japan there are purely—or more purely —technical problems, to be solved by experts in information and postindustrial technology, with a modest input from citizens. This is not so in the United States.

Consider some issues in the field of pollution. Perhaps the greatest contributor to air pollution is the automobile. One approach to this problem is devices on automobiles which suppress pollutants, regular inspections of automobiles to be sure that they contain these devices, the elimination from the roads of older automobiles that are not so equipped. The effect of such measures is first to increase the price of new cars, second to increase the cost of running cars, and third to eliminate from the roads or to make illegal the cheapest cars. Inevitably this increase in the price of new and old cars falls with the most severe effect on those poorest. Inevitably, this means it falls more heavily on the black population. A good part of this population is dependent on automobiles to get to work; it is well known that one problem in matching up low-skilled blacks with available jobs is that these jobs are increasingly outside the city and not on public transportation routes. But the reduction of the polluting characteristics of cars will make them more expensive for those who need them most to get to work.

This relationship is fortunately at this point one that is better known to engineers and cost-benefit analysts than to black community leaders. While the latter play no role in the fight on pollution—they seem to realize that this is after all a middle class and thus disproportionately a white issue—they are often aware of other conflicts of interests, as they see them, between white middle-class reformers and poor blacks. Consider another technical issue where moral considerations come into play. In recent years information on birth control has been spread among welfare families and the laws against abortion have been weakened (as against earlier years, when to suggest birth control to a welfare mother was taboo in most of the country and abortion was strictly illegal). It has become ever more evident that the large families of the poor, white or black, are an obstacle to their efforts at economic improvement. Under various governmental programs, birth control clinics have been opened in slum areas. In black areas, these have been opposed by black militants, one of whose favorite charges is that of "genocide." They see the new access to the information and techniques of birth control for black women as a form of genocide by the white power structure (and indeed, in most cases the doctors and voluntary workers in these clinics are white; there are too few black doctors and voluntary workers for the facts to be different). While the black militant protests against family-planning programs in black areas have been publicized, I don't believe they have been really effective. Black women do want these services and the birth-rate among them is dropping. Nevertheless, consider the effect of

140

such protests on those who propose opening such projects in the hope of reducing the pressure created on city social services by large numbers of new babies, many born to unmarried mothers, who may immediately become a charge on the welfare rolls, and on the health and welfare services, and who will shortly be added to the preschools and schools. Certainly the protests inhibit to some extent the expansion of such programs. Admittedly, everywhere family-planning programs come up against religious, moral, and political conflicts. But in American cities the conflict unhappily pits one race against the other, at a time when race is at the base of some of the most severe city problems.

Having said this, one must also point out that in problem areas such as pollution and transportation which are most remote from racial issues, we have the best chance of launching large and valuable programs of physical improvement in American cities. New programs of control of water pollution will benefit all. New programs of public transportation to replace cars on the roads will benefit all—and will perhaps benefit the poor more than the middle classes.

Let me point to one other area where technical improvements in urban life are possible, but where inevitably racial considerations play an enormous role, and that is the area of housing and planning. Obviously technical improvements in building are possible—improvements that will reduce the cost of housing and thus make available larger, newer, and more satisfactory housing units for people in cities. But in the field of housing, one comes up against the question of *location*—houses, alas, as against cars, must be placed on a permanent physical site. This raises all the questions involved in race again: Where are blacks to live, and where whites? I think the problems of interracial living in this country have been drastically reduced where middle-class whites and middle-class blacks are involved. But publicly supported housing, housing for the poor, will have a disproportionate share of blacks, since black families contribute heavily to the poor. The question of the location of housing

141

projects, which means the inflow of black and poor, thus becomes a very tense one. The housing project will have large numbers of children. They will crowd the schools, some of the children will beat or rob white children, the adolescents will prey on older people, some of the youths will contribute to more serious crime statistics. Is the resistance to housing projects resistance to the black or the poor? Does the resistance stem from the fact that poor blacks contribute disproportionately to crime or that the poor are generally black? It is hard to disentagle the various roots of resistance. In any case, this reality has made the issue of *where* to place housing in American cities far more serious than those to which information and technology can well contribute such as how to build. This issue has meant, for example, that urban renewal in most American cities has come to a halt.

The urban renewal programs which began in American cities after 1953 were designed to assist the process of replacing old inner cities' properties—residential, business, and industrial—with new ones. The new buildings were to be suited to the contemporary city, with better automobile access and superior technical facilities. They would, it was hoped, retain the tax-paying middle-class families in the center city by providing better residential and cultural facilities for them. The new structures would replace decaying slums. For such an enterprise, it seemed worthwhile to commit federal funds and the power of eminent domain to assemble property.

This account, which is more or less the kind of account on the basis of which urban renewal became a national program, leaves out the racial term that must be placed into all American urban equations. Urban renewal was almost immediately dubbed "Negro removal"; inevitably, the older slum areas that were to be cleared were disproportionately black. The properties that replaced them, because they were to be predominantly middle class, would have fewer blacks (though the middle-class developments built under urban renewal are generally the most successful examples of interracial housing in the cities in which they were built).

An obvious answer to this problem, of course, was to relocate the black and other poor residents of the central-city slums into adequate housing in other locations. But this raised a number of problems, again for the most part with an important racial element. If it was intended to build federally subsidized housing for the relocatees, legally, this housing had to be built within city borders; as housing for blacks it would not be acceptable in white suburbs. Even within the city, it would not be acceptable in white areas, or in mixed white-black middle-class areas, for after the 1950s housing projects developed a reputation as centers of crime and immoral living, and middle-class areas did not want them. Thus the housing projects were built either in the former slums where, to take account of high land values they had to be built as very high structures, or in rather out-of-the-way and distant places poorly served with public transportation and other facilities. The public housing projects of both kinds developed a bad reputation. A recent study argues that high-rise buildings made crime easier because of the extensive unguarded interior spaces such as in elevators, long corridors. In any case, families always knew the high-rises were bad for family living. How could a mother on the eighteenth floor keep in touch with her children playing on the ground? In the distant areas where some low-rent housing projects were located, the new tenants often felt they had been confined in a new black ghetto, and responded with anger and resentment, often expressed by attacks on firemen and policemen, and damage to property.

In New York City, Mayor Lindsay, accepting the advice of some of his housing advisors, decided that public housing must be built in middle-income areas, on "scattered sites," to overcome the depressing environmental effects of the old slums, and the newer, undeveloped outlying or bypassed areas. One such project was to be built in a middle-income area of New York, Forest Hills, and created one of the fiercest political storms of his administration. The middle-class residents already there—mostly white and Jewish, but actually with representatives of all races—protested to the point of violence. The project had to be cut in half, which, in view of the price of land, will raise the cost of each unit to about $60,000, far more than the cost of the housing which the ordinary resident of New York, who does not live in public housing, can afford.

It would be too depressing to continue the litany. The point is clear: the worst problems of our large cities cannot, it appears, be aided by new advances in information and post-industrial technology; those that can may not be able to utilize the new information and technology. In both cases, one important reason is the racial conflict in American cities; another is the buildup of the powerful municipal unions with their interest in maintaining things as they are.

What is the fundamental source of these conflicts, which we see in so many areas of urban life? (I have not discussed them in a number of areas, for example, in those of welfare and education, but they are just as intense in these areas as in those of crime and housing.) In one sense, after all, the American city is not unique. Every great city takes in migrants from the countryside, people with limited or no skills, of low literacy or none, immigrants incapable of speaking the language. These people, unable to enter the local economy at decent wages, will take the worst jobs and the worst housing, will form a disproportionate burden on social and health and protection services, will man the underworld and provide many of its customers and victims. How does what is happening in New York and Chicago differ from what is happening in London and Paris and Tokyo? How does race enter in to complicate the problem of urbanization which all growing cities deal with?

The new population that comes into American cities from smaller cities or rural background is in large measure black. A substantial part is white, and the white poor of the Middle West, stemming from Appalachia, are often not different from black migrants in their lack of skills, propensity toward large families, susceptibility to family breakdown, involvement in crime, and in their conflict with the settled population. Undoubtedly, however, the factor of race brings in new and sharper problems. First of all, the black has been subject to slavery and fierce prejudice and discrimination. How much of the remaining prejudice and discrimination he faces in the northern and western city is owing to his poverty and his social habits, and how much to his race, is still a matter of research and conjecture. Undoubtedly race alone, and the racial prejudice of Americans, explains a good deal. But we must add a number of other elements. The black is aware of his position as a *wronged* member of American society. As such, and in particular in recent years, he makes strong and insistent demands on the society's political and social agencies, demands fully justified by his position as a full citizen of that society and as one who has been subjected in various degrees to *official* wrongs. These demands may be found in all forms and at all levels—in the older civic organizations of blacks such as the NAACP and the National Urban League, in leaders who enter the traditional political parties, Democratic and Republican, and in a newer group of neighborhood and street leaders who are more radical than either the national civic organizations or the elected political representatives. Finally, and most unfortunately, these demands have another existence, at the lowest level, as a form of justification of criminal assault on the white population.

In Europe, where much of the dirty work of the cities is also increasingly done by immigrants, often colored, the migrants are aware of the fact that they can make few political demands on the society—they are probably not citizens, they may be temporary workers, and they do not think of themselves as the *victims* of the society in which they work (though Algerians in Paris and Yugoslavians in Germany might conceivably with some justification take that attitude). Thus they do not place the city in a situation of political and social crisis. In Japan, on the other hand, the new migrant to the city comes with a good education. He is literate and Japanese society is almost as open to him as to the urban youth of the same age. He does not see himself as the victim of urban Japanese society and does not declare war on it.

Thus the position of the American urban black is different. He combines the low skill level and low literacy of the migrant worker in Europe, with the sense of full participation in society of the migrant worker in Japan. It is an explosive combination.

Research has shown that the migrant black workers are on the whole the most docile and willing; it is they who still make up the substantial number of houseworkers, handymen, janitors, and the like. It is the urban black, born and raised in the city, who is the angriest and most likely participant in riots and in crime.

Here we must introduce a second element to explain the particularity of the race problem in the American city: the second and third and later generations are as visible as the first. If there is discrimination and prejudice, the second generation will be as victimized as the first, and for him Southern mores and reactions have been left far behind. (They have been left behind in the South as well, for the most part.) The generational disadvantages of poor education, large families, low skills, broken families, are also passed down to him and, as a full member of the society politically who does not benefit from it as much as others economically, his resentment is heightened. The result, as any dweller of a large American city may report, is not good.

Let us add to our story a few additional elements: in the Northeast a substantial part of the poor urban population is Puerto Rican. The Puerto Rican, coming from a former colony of the United States, bears potentially the same heritage as the black—a full citizen, on the one hand (the Puerto Rican can vote the day he sets foot in the continental United States, and need not demonstrate literacy in English to do so, as must other immigrants), and one with a load of substantial disadvantages on the other hand. In any case, the pattern of black resentment has now been passed on to the Puerto Rican, too. In Southwestern cities we find another large group among the poor, the Mexican-Americans. These also possess a heritage that encourages resentment: they live in lands conquered from Mexico, they are full citizens, and they suffer economic and other disadvantages. Discrimination is undoubtedly stronger against blacks than Puerto Ricans and Mexican-Americans, but all form part of the same chorus of demands and contribute, in varying measure, to the problems of the American city.

It is hard to find a Japanese equivalent. Koreans and *Burakumin* in some measure form such an equivalent. But their numbers are smaller, they are not racially distinct from the rest of the Japanese population, and undoubtedly there are other substantial differences.

There are postindustrial musings, analyses, and predictions for the American city. But oddly enough racial conflict is not a matter that is attractive to futurists. There is not a single reference to race in Hermann Kahn's and Anthony Wiener's otherwise impressive *The Year 2000*. If there were, one feels that the somewhat optimistic perspective of that book would have had to be muted.

The fact that America has race problems will not stop the onward rush of new technologies, of a postindustrial society with a knowledge base. Can the American mayor—or someone who stands in his position—see some contribution to his problems from these potential developments? It is revealing that Mayor Lindsay has strongly encouraged the New York City Rand Institute and strongly defended new techniques in city government. The Rand Institute is now I believe the largest urban research agency in the world. Mayor Lindsay has hoped to find ways of making New York City services more efficient. The budget in his seven years in office has tripled, going beyond the astonishing figure of $10 billion. The new analyses and new information-handling techniques proposed by the New York City Rand Institute have suggested ways of increasing the efficiency of fire, sanitation, and police departments, have suggested new approaches to housing policy (which it would take me too far afield to analyze, but which in this case do not involve any "futurist" component) and the New York City Bureau of the Budget, following the path laid down by the prestigious agency of the same name in Washington, has grown faster probably than any other department of city government. Despite this, the actual crises of Mayor Lindsay's administration escape the capacity of even the best-funded and best-supported information-oriented agencies to grapple with the problems of New York. Organized city employees on the one hand (who have made New York City employees the best paid of their type in the country), and racial conflicts on the other have made the heaviest drain on the time and energy of the mayor. I suspect other mayors would report a very similar story.

Futurist thinking about cities has, for three-quarters of a century now, concentrated on one course as a way of improving city life; I refer to the New Town, or Garden City, as it was called when Ebenezer Howard invented the phrase. If one thinks of a large-scale solution to the problems raised by large cities, almost inevitably, in every nation, and in every time and place, the notion of the garden city, the new town, or a system of new towns, comes to mind. For the generic problems of large cities are those of congestion in transportation, accompanying pollution of air and water, and distance from countryside for leisure and recreation for most of the population. The United States has probably been more backward than most countries in undertaking this route to an alleviation of city problems. Ebenezer Howard started two garden cities in Great Britain with voluntary support; and after World War II, the first large program of new town was launched there. New towns are still being founded and must certainly be accounted one of the successes of British social policy. In Japan, too, where for twenty years the growth of the giant city of Tokyo has dominated urban analysis, there has been an accompanying series of programs to relocate population or at least new urban growth into new towns some distance from Tokyo, or on the Pacific Coast, which has not shared in the incredible growth of postwar Japan. Prime Minister Tanaka, in a best-selling book that preceded his accession to office, reemphasized this objective.

I do not mean to suggest that the New Town is all that future-minded city thinkers have come up with. We have seen many fabulous proposals for cities in which elements are piled up on each other like parts of a giant erector set. In these megastructural responses to urban physical growth we see efforts to deal with congestion by structural innovations that increase density but in frameworks in which interior lines of communication and transportation reduce congestion. The model elements for the megastructure are the urban elevator and the telephone. One of the most remarkable examples of these megastructures is the John Hancock 100-story building in Chicago, where indeed there are people who live on the 85th floor and commute to work on the 35th, and in so doing add nothing to the congestion of Chicago. But it is the rare individual who can afford to do this, or wishes to. Solutions such as the John Hancock Building, and the awesome proposals for Tokyo of Kenzo Tange, cannot be considered means of improving city life for the great majority of city dwellers. These after all are families with children who do not want to be isolated from ground and greenery. To build huge concrete urban platforms from which all the parts of a city spring is to my mind a very partial solution to a partial problem.

It is the new town that is still the basic instrument for futurist urban reform, supplemented by more rapid transportation to the city, and richer and fuller communication (the three-dimensional communication of cultural programs, and so forth). It is interesting to review the American experience with the new town.

In the early 1960s, as the suburban explosion continued, some corporations and land developers conceived of more than Levittowns—they wanted developments that were more of an independent city and contributed thus more to the solution of megalopolitan problems. A spate of new towns was launched. A few survive in particular, Reston and Columbia. At this time, the Ford Foundation commissioned a study of what the New Town could contribute to the solution of American urban problems. The resultant book by Edward Eichler and Marshall Kaplan, expresses once again the dilemma of American urban futurism. Eichler and Kaplan had no reason to disapprove of new towns. But they had to ask themselves the key question of American urbanism: What would new towns do for the race problem? Sadly, they decided, nothing.

The new towns would have to draw from the more prosperous parts of urban populations—those who could afford new houses or apartments, or long commutation trips. This had been, after all, the experience of new towns in England and is probably the experience of new towns in Japan. The blacks would form a very small part of the new towns. Drawing off the more prosperous and disproportionately white populations, the new towns would increase the black concentrations in the older cities. Drawing off the new factories and office buildings, they would deepen the economic crises of the older cities left to the blacks. Could a proportionate number of blacks as well as whites be attracted to the new towns? Only by the most costly efforts. There would have to be a substantial investment in heavily subsidized housing. Since the success of the new town depended on its attracting a substantial share of families of full tax-paying abilities, one would have to be concerned with the impact on their decision to move to the new town of an advertised commitment to have in the new town a substantial share of inner-city blacks. If one drew off from the city blacks with good or stable jobs, one would only increase the proportion of blacks living on welfare, and who are thus a burden to the city. As it is, something like one-third or two-fifths of the black population of northeastern cities are currently on welfare. Would one want to increase this proportion?

150

The fact is, despite this analysis which suggested a gloomy prognosis for the contribution of new towns to either racial integration or the financial problems of older cities, the American government did move in the direction of supporting a small new town program. Grants and loans were awarded to selected developers who accepted certain government requirements, namely to provide housing for various income levels so that low-paid workers could live in the new town and adopt measures promoting racial integration. Whether the difficulties to which Eichler and Kaplan pointed some years ago can really be overcome remains an open question.

Meanwhile, the mayors of older cities are not happy with the new towns because of their capacity to draw off middle-income residents, as well as tax-paying factories and office buildings. Indeed, contemplating the potential reality of a new town on the Hackensack Meadows across the Hudson River from New York, one high New York official has proposed that cities should have veto power over the building of new towns in their vicinities. Of course, as federal revenue-sharing spreads and a higher share of urban revenues becomes independent of the property-tax base, this opposition may decline.

In talking of the American city, we have focused on the largest cities and have drawn many of our examples from the very largest, New York. What we have said is true, more or less, for many other large cities—Chicago, Philadelphia, Detroit, to name a few. To focus on these cities is to see the urban crisis in a rather advanced and serious form. We have not concentrated on the most pathological cases. Newark, with its rapid abandonment of property and its near bankruptcy would be a worse case. Nor on the other hand have we looked at middle-sized American cities, such as Tulsa or Indianapolis, where in many ways things are better and a pleasanter urban environment is maintained. Not long ago a book was published on the safe places in the United States (those cities in which crime was not a problem) and the authors found quite a few, though they were of course the smaller cities.

What of the fate of the largest American cities? I have concentrated on pathology—unfortunately, the city-dweller cannot help but become aware of this when he thinks of his city—and have found it difficult to see how the revolution in information gathering and processing in the postindustrial society will make rapid and effective reductions in this pathology. I have pointed out, however, that we do find progress in the management of city problems. Many believe that if we put the resources into research and development on urban management that we have on such projects as getting to the moon we would make much more rapid progress. Since our urban problems are rooted in the inevitably slow urbanization of large new populations of distinct racial background with a disastrous social history, I believe there are limits to the usefulness or applicability of new information to improve our cities. This is not to downgrade the importance of work on the information needs and technology of urban life. Some urban problems, those in particular stemming from congestion and pollution, are very much the same, whatever the social origins of our urban population, and should be attacked more effectively, whatever the state of the urban racial crisis.

But this caution on my part should not be interpreted as despair. It is my expectation that the crisis in race relations in American cities is not a permanent one and will be moderated in the future. Indeed, it has already shown some improvement since its peak in the years of the summer racial crises, 1964 to 1968, in Watts, Newark, Detroit, and Washington. The year 1968, already five years old, was the last with major riots of the black population of American cities. Many of us feared that these riots would be succeeded by guerilla warfare, as many of the new urban black leaders threatened. There were serious incidents in Cleveland, Chicago, New York, and elsewhere, but now, it seems as if we may well have passed the peak of urban guerilla warfare, too. The 1970 census reported what many other statistics had indicated: huge increases in the number of blacks in white-collar and professional jobs; huge increases in the number of blacks in white colleges; a substantial narrowing of the gap in income between whites and blacks; and most surprisingly, a near equivalence in the income of young black and white couples in the North and West. It is on these younger blacks that programs of recent years have been concentrated.

But the signs are mixed. For while the number of blacks in good and secure jobs rose far more rapidly than among whites, there was at the same time an enormous increase in broken black families and in blacks living on welfare. These contradictory trends moved together, and we may, by extrapolating one or the other, predict either a narrowing or widening of the gap between white and black. Whatever improvements have been made have resulted from black political and extrapolitical action, followed by important federal legislation and the establishment of large federal programs in the fields of voter registration, education, employment, work-training, and so on. These new efforts are by now institutionalized through the establishment of permanent federal and state agencies, and it is hard to see any falling back from the advances that have been marked in these fields.

Nevertheless, it is illusory to assume that the state of black-white relations in the United States depends solely on the objective situation of blacks in education, in jobs, in politics. If it did, we could look forward optimistically to improved conditions. The state of black-white relations is in part dependent on the objective realities of the black situation. It is even more dependent, however, on the arts of politics exercised by both black and white, at federal, state, and local levels, arts which are designed to advance the interests of groups and to find compromises with which groups can live. It is because, in the end, the state of black-white relations is so fully dependent on politics, and politics in any basic sense is so little affected by technological and informational change, that one must look at the fate of American cities as very much governed by men as they are, rather than by men as they will be when armed with the new knowledge of the postindustrial society. I look forward eagerly to what the informational revolution of the postindustrial society will permit us to do in our cities; but whatever it permits us to do, it will not bring about the basic alteration in the situation of white and black that is at the heart of so many of our city problems. Only men as they are, with whatever weapons political intelligence suggests, can alter that situation.

Chapter Seven

An Approach to the Measurement of the Levels of Welfare in Tokyo

Ken'ichi Tominaga

In the twenty-five years following World War II, the Japanese economy has grown at a rapid rate, and with it the real income of the Japanese household has also increased. On the average, the disposable income for a Japanese household has shown a 9.5 percent annual increase for the eighteen-year period between 1954 and 1972. As a result the standard of living—food, clothing, housing, and so forth—has improved greatly. For example, the rate of diffusion of consumer durable goods, many of which had not spread at all in 1950, has increased to the point that 61.1 percent of Japanese households owned color television sets in 1972, 91.6 percent owned electric refrigerators, and 30.1 owned automobiles. In addition, the increase in daily consumption of animal protein, which went from 27.0 grams in 1950 to 31.7 grams in 1967, can be seen as an example of the way in which the Japanese diet has greatly improved.[1]

155

One might suppose, therefore, that an increasing number of the Japanese people would take satisfaction in this growing affluence. A recent national survey does show that most Japanese who receive higher-than-average personal incomes are relatively satisfied with the general state of their lives, but a significant percentage of those who receive lower incomes are not (see Table 7-1). Thus the trend over the years toward a higher average personal income has not brought a corresponding increase in the percentage of Japanese who find their lives satisfactory; that percentage seems to remain relatively stationary. In 1959, when a national sample of the population was asked whether their lives had become more comfortable in the past year, 12 percent answered yes; 59 percent said that things remained about the same; 26 percent answered that life had become more difficult; and 3 percent did not know. When the same question was asked again in 1971, the percentage of each response had scarcely changed; the vast majority still found life getting worse or at least no better (see Table 7-2). Yet during this same period, the average annual personal income of the Japanese people had increased five times from $319 to $1,583.

Thus there does not seem to be a linear relationship between objective living standard—as measured, for example, in disposable income, housing, diet, and durable consumer goods—and level of satisfaction as a subjective psychological fact. Clearly, satisfaction is not determined solely by the objective standard of living. Even a multivariate regression analysis of the same data as shown in Table 7-1 suggests that high income is not the principal or even a very important explanatory variable of a people's sense of well-being.[2]

Why is this so? Why is it that the rise of income level on a national scale does not directly produce a rise in the level of satisfaction? One explanation is that the level of aspiration is a mediating psychological factor. The more goods and services the economy produces, the more each individual wants. According to reference group theory, one's levels of

Table 7-1
Question: "Are You Satisfied or Dissatisfied with the General State of Your Life?"

Annual Income (10,000 Yen)	Satisfied	Neither	Dis- satisfied	Don't Know	Total
Less than 60	45.7	22.3	29.6	2.4	100.0
60- 90	45.7	23.6	28.6	2.0	100.0
90-120	50.8	22.1	25.9	1.2	100.0
120-150	56.1	23.0	19.7	1.1	100.0
150-180	56.7	22.4	20.1	0.8	100.0
180-210	61.6	19.9	18.0	0.4	100.0
210-240	62.8	19.8	16.4	0.9	100.0
240-270	61.5	22.6	15.6	0.3	100.0
270-300	68.0	16.4	15.6	0.0	100.0
More than 300	69.7	17.0	12.5	0.9	100.0

Source: Economic Planning Agency, *Report on National Preference Survey*, 1972 (1972 National Samples, N = 10,468).

aspiration are formed in relation to the attainments of other people. Thus, as the living standard of those with whom one compares oneself rises, so does one's own level of aspiration tend to rise and the "standard package" of goods and services an individual requires tends to expand.[3] Of course this does not mean that the economic growth was in vain. A well-known psychological principle is that changes in levels of aspiration tend to be irreversible and to gather momentum. When, as now, people regard it as natural for the "standard package" to increase annually, there is little doubt that a sudden halt in economic growth, causing a frustration of these rising expectations, would result in serious psychological panic.

Another explanation for the gap between the "objective" improvement of the economy and the "subjective" level of satisfaction is the change in values which increasing affluence brings. As one becomes equipped with consumer durable goods and other conveniences, he begins to think more about other aspects of his living conditions: the adequacy of public services, social security systems, and educational

Table 7-2

Question: "Compared with Last Year, Is Life at Your House More Comfortable?" (in Percentages)

	1959	1960	1961	1962	1963	1964	1965	1966	1967	1968	1969	1971
More Comfortable	12	14	18	16	14	10	7	7	8	8	8	12
About the Same	59	65	61	56	58	56	51	50	60	59	64	59
More Difficult	26	17	17	24	23	31	38	42	30	30	26	25
Don't Know	3	4	4	4	5	3	4	1	2	3	2	4
	—	—	—	—	—	—	—	—	—	—	—	—
	100	100	100	100	100	100	100	100	100	100	100	100

Source: The Prime Minister's Office, *The Monthly Public Opinion Poll*, October 1971, p. 6. (The poll lacks 1970 data.)

facilities; the cleanliness of the air and other elements in his natural environment; and the vitality of the human relations within his community—precisely those conditions which are not necessarily improved by a high rate of economic growth. Accordingly, when people obtain private cars, they soon realize that the roads are heavily congested. When people can afford a holiday tour, they find that industrialization and urbanization have destroyed beautiful seashores and hills. When people wish to do something socially, they notice that there is no congenial community around them anymore. These new lacks tend to offset the gratification obtained from a rising income and widen the gap between the degree of economic prosperity and that of psychological satisfaction. It is in this context that people begin to argue that economic growth is one thing and "welfare" is another.

Over the past several years emphasis on economic growth, defined by the rate of increase of the GNP has been conspicuously strong in Japan. Now, however, the rise of new dissatisfactions is leading more and more Japanese to realize the GNP is simply an indicator of economic activity and does not measure the noneconomic aspects of social life. A need for a new "social indicator" has been felt, a new standard by which the level of "social welfare" can be measured as effectively as the economy.[4]

Social scientists in all advanced countries have felt this need, but a social indicator is not yet an established tool. It is not difficult, of course, to gather data on such social facts as the number of television sets owned per family or the square feet of park space available per individual or the rate of admissions to universities. The problem arises when we try to relate these data to each other systematically and reduce them to a common measure so that they can be synthesized into a single index or at least several subindices. Monetary measures, so useful to the economist in measuring GNP, will not serve in this case, since such items as levels of housing and other living conditions in kind, levels of public facilities and other related "nonmarketable" goods, and levels of

159

unpolluted natural environment must be included; and these are not reducible to monetary terms. This is because the social indicator is not an economic concept. It must measure the conditions of "social welfare," or it might be better to say "societal welfare," by which I would mean the degree to which the members of a social system are equipped with the "social goods" that system can supply.[5]

One possible approach to the measurement of this social state might be to try to measure the level of psychic satisfaction which individuals find in a given social condition, however, such a micro or subjective approach confronts immediate difficulties.

One of these is the impossibility of comparing the psychic states of individuals interpersonnally, or of adding them arithmetically, to derive the psychic state of the social system as a whole, for like GNP, the social indicator we need must be a macro concept applicable to the social system, not the individual level. If we were to start from a micro or individual level we could not avoid the aggregation problem, which first came to light in the analysis of the concept of "utility" in economics. The neoclassical economic theorists, holding to a belief in utilitarian individualism, first suggested that a concept of social welfare could be derived from the micro, subjective concept of utility. A. C. Pigou, for example, assumed that individual utilities were comparable and that the welfare of the society could be derived by adding up the sum total of their individual utilities. But the theorists of the "new" welfare economics who came after him rejected these assumptions; and Kenneth Arrow has now conclusively demonstrated the logical fallacy in the neoclassicist's assumption.[6]

Moreover, it is not necessarily significant to relate a subjective variable like satisfaction to objective variable like the square measure of housing per person or the acreage of public parks. Mathematically, of course, it is practicable in a linear regression to make satisfaction a dependent variable and objective measures independent variables; but men's sentiments do not necessarily flow so straight forwardly in relation to their environment.

I suggest that we approach the problem by seeking to measure social welfare at the objective societal level without relating it directly to the subjective individual "utility" concept. To use the structural-functional terminology in sociology, the social system and the personality system are two different, distinct entities, and to regard the social system as an aggregate of personality systems (to wit, psychological reductionism) is impossible. Thus we should not commence with the personality system, but go directly to the social system.

Following Talcott Parsons, we will call the conditions necessary for a social system to support itself and grow the "functional prerequisites" of the social system. As Parsons has pointed out, one of the functional prerequisites of a social system is that it meet the needs of the personality systems of its individual members.[7] To this extent the functional prerequisites of the personality system and the social system are related. It must be noted, however, that this is not the only functional prerequisite of a social system; there are many others. In this regard, the situation is ideal when the need-gratification of the personality system coexists with the other functional prerequisites of the social system. In that case, the social system itself is functioning well and the people will not be dissatisfied. An example would be an industrial organization which is able both to realize a profit and to maintain high morale among its employees.

Here the problem is to determine a standard for judging whether functional needs are being met. Of course, because there cannot be an absolute standard, the problem is one of relative degree. I should like to propose two possible standards: one is the "welfare minimum point" (hereafter referred to as the M point) and the other is the "welfare fulfilling point" (hereafter referred to as the F point). As implied in the term, the M point is the minimum standard which the society must meet in order to achieve the minimum acceptable level of social welfare. The F point is the standard which, when met, will fulfill the aspirations for social welfare.

Whether or not the quantity of social goods—including not only goods with economic value but also other tangible and intangible resources which serve to gratify people's needs—is at the level necessary to ensure need gratification, is an evaluation to be made by the individual, and of course individuals have different levels of needs. However, when a consensus has been reached by a majority of a system's members, limiting the way in which social welfare is to evaluated to the limited boundaries, it is possible to define the M and F points. When such a consensus is not reached, the M and F points must remain undefined.

Since human needs are many and varied, social welfare can be thought of as being divided into many elements. Each of these elements corresponds to one of many different needs. We will call these elements the *components* of welfare, and define the sum of welfare as the weighted sum of its component parts.

A convenient measure of the level of welfare of a given component can now be constructed as a ratio of the amount by which the current quantity of a given component exceeds its M point to the amount the F point of that component exceeds the M point. This may be expressed in the following equation:

Component Welfare Indicator

$$= \frac{\text{Current quantity minus M Point}}{\text{F Point minus M Point}} \times 100 \qquad (7.1)$$

Let us take an example. Suppose in a particular society there are 1000 television sets. Suppose also that a survey reveals that the M point, that is, the minimum number of sets that would satisfy the majority of the people is 500 and that the F point, or number of sets which would meet the current aspir-

162

ations of most people is 2000, we might then derive the Component Welfare Indicator of television set ownership by the following equation:

Component Welfare Indicator (TV)

$$= \frac{1000 \text{ (Current)} - 500 \text{ (M)}}{2000 \text{ (F)} - 500 \text{ (M)}} = \frac{500}{1500} \times 100 = 33.3$$

Obviously, when the current quantity and the M point are the same, the index will equal zero, indicating the society's minimum satisfaction with the supply of this component; whereas when the current quantity and the F point are the same, the index will equal 100, indicating the society's full satisfaction.

Now it will be seen that if the Welfare Indicator of each component is weighted by a figure indicating the priority the public gives to that component, and that if these weighted measures are then added together, one can derive a comprehensive indicator of the social welfare of the society as follows:[8]

Social Welfare Indicator = Component Welfare Indicator
   × Component Relative Weight
   + sum of all other weighted component indicators   (7.2)

The validity of these concepts and formulations needs further testing, but they have already been applied with interesting results to the city of Tokyo this past year.

With the rapid growth of the Japanese economy, the environments of cities like Tokyo have seriously deteriorated. One of the main reasons for this is that industrialization has caused an overconcentration of the population in the preexisting urban areas. Thus housing conditions have wor-

163

sened; public facilities such as parks, water and sewage systems, and garbage disposal systems have become insufficient; per capita medical care is lacking; roads and transportation facilities are crowded and congested—in short, life in the cities has become difficult.

Despite this, however, it is still difficult to say that city life is on the whole worse than it was before. We previously defined "social welfare" as the state of satisfaction with the quantity of social goods offered by the social system. Social goods include both the material and nonmaterial resources corresponding to and satisfying the countless needs of human beings. Among the social goods there are some which have deteriorated because of industrialization and there are others which have improved. I have mentioned examples of those which have deteriorated; among those which have improved are personal income, durable consumer goods, life expectancy, employment opportunities, worker safety, education, the diffusion of devices such as the telephone, and so forth. It is therefore meaningless to say simply that social welfare has become worse; the problem is to determine the areas of social welfare which have deteriorated and the degree of their deterioration. What I shall relate below is a recent attempt at such an empirical study of Tokyo.[9]

The "social goods" which determine the level of "social welfare" are countless, and there is not yet a way to systematically organize and classify them with certainty. Furthermore, the basic units of measurement differ, depending on the goods involved. For example, the basic unit for measuring household income is money; living space or the size of public parks is measured by area; the number of medical or educational facilities per 10,000 people is measured by counting the people and the facilities, and so on. To solve these difficulties in performing a trend analysis it was necessary to take the following steps in measuring the level of social welfare of Tokyoites.

Step 1: Devise a category system to catalogue the various kinds of social goods.

Step 2: Devise a list of as many of the components of welfare as possible and divide them into appropriate categories.

Step 3: For each individual component, determine the M and F points as defined earlier.

Step 4: Using the equation (7.1) above, transform the actual quantities of the various components to a standardized measure of welfare.

Step 5: After deciding on the appropriate weights for the components, use the equation (7.2) above to compute each category as well as the entire aggregate of components making up the Social Welfare Indicator.

Let us begin with the first step. In discussing social indicators there is always the problem of how to organize the welfare categories, for there is as yet no established method of categorization. Looking at previous works on the subject, we came up with ten categories which we called the *domains* of welfare, crossed by three categories which we called the *divisions* of welfare. Cross-tabulating the divisions and the domains we came up with a table of thirty boxes (Table 7-3). The ten domains form the vertical axis of this table. This is a categorization of the many different aspects of human needs. On the horizontal axis welfare is divided into three divisions: individual life, living environment, and social control. The criterion for this classification was whether this particular aspect of welfare falls on the individual, the community, or the public sector. The indicator for "individual life" is concerned with both the conditions of the life of the private individual as well as that of the household. The division termed "living environment" has to do with the access to public facilities, the opportunity to enjoy public conveniences, and the general condition of aspects of the environment which the individual cannot provide for himself. "Social control" has to do with the level of welfare resources which the individual or the household alone cannot mobilize; in other words, those resources which can only be mobilized through the government.

As for the second step, we came up with some 250 items from various documents and data. Examining each for its representativeness, comprehensiveness, and adaptability to time-series analysis, we finally ended up with 180 items to serve as *components* in the social welfare indicator. Because it would take a great deal of space to present the entire list, I have given a representative sample for each of the thirty boxes in Table 7-3.

The third step, establishing the M and F points, was the central procedure of this research. As explained in their definition, the M and F points are the standards by which the state of social welfare is evaluated. In this case evaluation does not mean the kind of subjective judgment which differs between individuals, but an evaluation based on social norms which have been established by a certain degree of mutual agreement. To determine the standards for this evaluation, we consulted with various experts. In all we chose some fifty first-rate specialists—doctors, urban planners, economists, educators, and so forth from Tokyo's leading universities and research centers—and, using the Delphi method, had them reply to certain questions. Where there was a big discrepancy in their answers, we removed the item from the list, and in this way we eliminated 101 items from the 180, after which the M and F points for the remaining 79 were determined. Although I don't think it would have been impossible to base the M and F points on a random sample of ordinary people, I do think that the technical nature of the problem would have made this latter method more difficult.

Once the third step was reached, the remaining steps four and five only involve simple computation. It is necessary, however, to discuss the way in which the items were weighted for equation (7.2) above. It is possible to think of various ways in which the items could have been weighted, but we chose the method which was used in obtaining the results of a survey concerning the desires and demands of the people of Tokyo. This method is the same as that used by sociologists

Table 7-3
Categories and Examples of Components of Welfare

	Divisions of Welfare		
Domains of Welfare	Individual Life	Living Environment	Social Control
Income-Consumption	Per capita income	Per capita GNP	Per capita income of people on government pensions
Medical Care	Longevity	Number of hospital beds	Number of public health centers
Housing	Tatami mats per person	Δ Rent (private housing)	Diffusion of public water systems
Working Conditions	Δ Monthly working hours	Δ Work accidents	The rate of employment of middle and old aged as arranged through the employment security office
Leisure Time	Trips per month	Area of public parks	Number of public libraries
Education	% of college or junior college graduates	Δ Ratio of elementary school teachers to students	Number of grades in public specialty schools
Solidarity	Δ % of suicides	Δ Incidents of juvenile delinquency	Capacity of homes for the aged
Transportation-Communication	% of telephones	Δ Degree of traffic congestion	% of paved streets
Safety	% of people with life insurance	Δ Number of traffic accidents	% of arrests for criminal offenses
Natural Environment	—	Δ Degree of air pollution	Number of pollution control centers

Δ Indicates a minus indicator; in other words when the figure is large, peoples' needs are not being met.

167

to determine the relative prestige of occupations in occupational rankings. The result is that all the items are computed in such a way that the respective means equal unity.[10] (See Table 7-4)

The level of welfare measured through steps one through five are shown in Table 7-5 and Figure 7-1. These tables represent syntheses of the ten domains and three divisions respectively of social welfare. The figures within the same cells are the simple means, and the syntheses between the domains and divisions were done by taking the weights shown in Table 7-4.

From Table 7-5 and Figure 7-1 we can read the following: looking at the upper half of Table 7-5 or at Figure 7-1a, we see that most of the domains of welfare are below the M point; however, among the ten domains seven are rising annually, indicating that welfare is improving. Second, in Tokyo, working conditions, medical care, and education are fairly good; and income and public safety have also shown recent improvements. Third, the domains which have become worse are housing conditions, transportation, and the the natural environment. Among these, housing conditions have deteriorated the most. Although in 1965 transportation

Table 7-4
The Weights for Thirty Welfare Components

	Individual Life	Living Environment	Social Control
Income-Consumption	1.27	1.03	1.03
Medical Care	—[a]	1.02	1.26
Housing	1.02	1.01	1.04
Working Conditions	1.00	1.00	0.71
Leisure Time	0.90	0.66	0.91
Education	0.94	0.89	0.94
Solidarity	1.24	1.19	0.93
Transportation-Communication	0.63	0.83	0.95
Safety	—	1.21	1.08
Natural Environment	—	1.16	1.15

[a]There are three blanks because of the lack of appropriate data and/or doubtfulness of the representativeness of the indicator.

was second to medical care, it fell in the subsequent five years to position nine in 1970. In this graph, however, transportation and communication have been put together, which means that because communication has improved, the actual extent of the deterioration of transportation is concealed. If transportation is taken alone, the line plunges downward at an even faster rate. As for the natural environment, even though there is a slight improvement since the time when a lot was heard over newspaper and television about polluted water and air, the level is still very low. On the other hand, the level of medical care ranks high; but because it has shown little improvement, it has actually become worse, and in 1969 working conditions took over first place.

Looking at Figure 7-1b and the lower half of Table 7-5, we first see that individual living conditions have improved, reflecting such things as the increases in per capita income, longevity, and the diffusion of pleasure traveling. Moreover, the standard itself has been above the M point since 1965. Second, social control, which is based on government policies, has improved but is still below the M point. Third, among the three divisions, the living environment is the worst; and with the improvements in the other two divisions, the trend has been toward an increasing gap between this division and the other two. This gap will be called the "welfare gap." Recalling the definitions of the individual life and living environment divisions, it is clear that this gap is a result of the difference between the kinds of welfare the individual can obtain through his own efforts (through activities in the market place) and those which can be obtained only through the community (the "nonmarketable" items). Clearly, economic growth raises the individual's standard of living, but without raising the standard of the nonmarketable aspects of "living environment" the gap increases. The third division, social control, is in a position to close this gap inasmuch as it involves the mobilization by the government of welfare resources; however, the actual situation is such that, even though social control improves annually, the gap remains because the absolute level is so low.

169

Figure 7-1. The Time-Series Trend of the Social Welfare Indicators

a: The Trend for the Domains

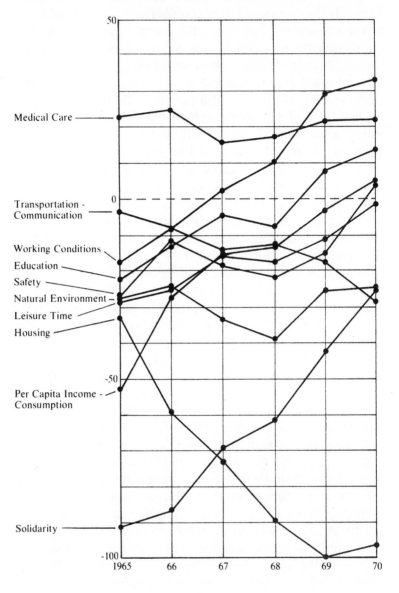

b: The Trend for the Divisions

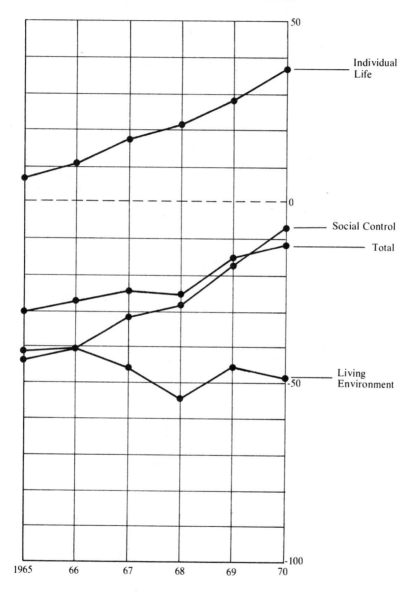

Table 7-5
A Time-Series Table of the Domains, Divisions, and Sum Totals of Social Welfare

		1965	1966	1967	1968	1969	1970
	Per Capita income and consumption	− 53.3	− 28.0	− 15.8	− 13.5	− 3.0	5.1
	Medical Care	22.6	25.0	16.8	17.8	22.3	22.9
	Housing	− 32.6	− 59.5	− 72.9	− 89.7	− 100.5	− 96.9
Domains	Working Conditions	− 17.5	− 8.5	2.9	10.6	30.0	33.6
of	Leisure Time	− 28.7	− 25.0	− 16.0	− 17.3	10.3	1.7
Welfare	Education	− 22.0	− 12.1	− 4.8	− 7.3	9.1	14.3
	Solidarity	− 91.4	− 87.0	− 69.5	− 61.4	42.7	− 25.6
	Transportation—Communication	− 3.9	− 8.3	− 13.0	− 12.1	− 18.1	− 28.9
	Safety	− 26.4	− 10.9	− 18.4	− 21.8	− 14.0	4.8
	Natural Environment	− 27.8	− 24.1	− 33.3	− 39.3	− 26.0	− 25.7
Divisions	Individual Life	3.3	11.0	17.9		28.1	37.2
of	Living Environment	− 41.5	− 40.3	− 45.5	− 53.8	− 46.5	− 48.5
Welfare	Social Control	− 44.4	− 40.4	− 31.9	− 27.8	− 17.4	− 7.2
	Total	− 30.3	− 27.0	− 24.0	− 24.8	− 16.4	− 11.0

In determining the welfare standard for the people of Tokyo, the housing, transportation, and natural environment domains presented particular difficulties, especially under the division of the living environment. Because the three divisions and ten domains in Table 7-5 and Figure 7-1 are shown independently, the connections between them are not clear; however, the results of cross-tabulation (omitted here for the economy of the space) showed that among the thirty cells the combinations of housing-living environment, housing-social control, transporation-living environment, and natural environment-living environment respectively are the four which are the worst. And these are none other than the four items which are usually taken to reveal the true extent to which social welfare has deteriorated with the high rate of economic growth.

Since Daniel Bell coined the phrase "post-industrial society" several years ago, it has almost become an established concept. I still feel doubtful about the prefix *post-* since most elements which characterize the so-called postindustrial society are not so fundamentally different from those subsumed under the general conception of the "industrial society."[11] Apart from that, however, I would like to agree with one of his central theses, that is, that the postindustrial society will come to rely less on simple "machine technology" and more on "intellectual technology." And I would suggest that the social indicator is an example of this new "intellectual technology."[12]

Seen from the viewpoint of the change of the distributional pattern of the work force, Japan today is trending toward a postindustrial transformation. As I have analyzed elsewhere,[13] in the period from 1955 to 1970, the trend in the changing structure of the Japanese work force has centered around the rapid increase in blue-collar workers, particularly semiskilled workers, which is typical in the development of manufacturing industries. Although the rate of increase of blue-collar workers has started to decline, unlike the situation in America, the increase in Japan is still fairly rapid. On

173

the other hand, the rapid increase of white-collar workers also continues; here the increase is mainly among office workers and salesmen, not among professionals. From this standpoint, it seems to be too early to say that Japan is on the verge of becoming a postindustrial society.

However, in the last two or three years the appearance of a new generation which takes economic prosperity for granted is causing a change in values. This new generation, born after the war, tends to possess the values of a postindustrial society. For example, they are rather indifferent to the fruits of production, and they don't put as high a value on diligence as did the former generation. Certainly, some of the unique characteristics of the postindustrial society are starting to appear.

In the analysis above, we have seen that while the household income of Tokyoites has increased and the goods which the private individual can purchase in the marketplace are plentiful, the deterioration of public facilities and the living environment is keenly felt, and the dissatisfactions stemming from the welfare gap have increased. Because of this, residents in large cities are starting to reconsider the pattern of rapid economic growth which has prevailed up until the present. On the other hand, residents of smaller cities or rural villages are still dissatisfied with their small incomes and desire the rate of economic growth to continue. Akin to the problem of the disparity of the advantages between advanced and underdeveloped countries on the international level, there is a problem of the differences in advantages between advanced and underdeveloped regions within Japan.[14]

Thus, in the large cities which are on the threshold of the postindustrial society, the problem is to decrease the welfare gap; while in the smaller cities and the villages, the problem is to decrease the differences existing between them and the big cities. This is the situation of the welfare problem in modern Japan. Because these problems cannot be neglected, it is now thought that the central government will have to tighten its control and take a more active role in the management of the total social system. Of course, when control is tightened the problem of power arises. However, control in this sense must be taken to mean technocratic control based on specialized knowledge, not personal, arbitrary power. If this is achieved, the postindustrial society will, as Daniel Bell suggests, shift its reliance from simple "machine technology" to "intellectual technology." Thus, a device for measuring the welfare level in terms of the social indicators discussed in this chapter will become an increasingly necessary tool for social planning in the coming postindustrial age.

Notes

1. These statistics are from the People's Livelihood Research Center, ed., *Kokumin seikatsu tōkei nenpō* [The people's livelihood statistical Yearbook](Tokyo: Shiseido, 1972].

2. Income ranked only seventeenth out of thirty-three independent variables associated. Research Committee on National Preference Survey, *Nihonjin no Manzokudo* [Degree of satisfaction of the Japanese people](Tokyo: Shiseidō, 1972), p. 117.

3. David Riesman with H. Roseborough, "Careers and Consumer Behavior," in *Abundance for What? and Other Essays,* (New York: Doubleday, 1964), pp. 113-37.

4. R. A. Bauer, ed., *Social Indicators*, (Cambridge, Mass.: M.I.T. Press, 1966); U.S. Department of Health, Education and Welfare, *Toward a Social Report* (Washington, D.C.: GPO, 1969); Daniel Bell, "The Idea of Social Report," *The Public Interest,* Spring 1969, pp. 72-84; Ken'ichi Tominaga, "Shakai shihyō to shakai keikaku", in *Sangyō shakai no dōtai* [Dynamics of industrial society](Tokyo: Tōyō Keizai, 1973), Ch. 11.

5. This concept of "social welfare" must be understood as a theoretically parallel concept with "economic welfare"

175

in A. C. Pigou, *The Economics of Welfare*, London: Macmillan, 1920 (1938 ed.), p. 10. "Social goods" is a generalized concept expanded from "economic goods." It corresponds to the "welfare resources" to be discussed later. Social goods are divided between economic goods, "relational goods," cultural goods, etc. See Ken'ichi Tominaga, *Shakai hendō no riron* [Theories of social change](Tokyo: Iwanami Shoten, 1965), Ch. II.

6. K. J. Arrow, *Social Choice and Individual Values* 2nd ed. (New York: John Wiley, 1963).

7. Talcott Parsons, *The Social System* (Glencoe, Ill.: Free Press, 1951), pp. 26-36.

8. To arrange the above mathematically, I will express the current quantity of the components of welfare as Zi, the M point as Mi and the F point as Fi. The appropriate level of the welfare components Ii can be expressed as:

$$Ii = \frac{Zi - Mi}{Fi - Mi}$$

Here the numerator indicates the degree that the current quantity of the welfare components exceeds the M point, while the denominator expresses the range between the F and M points. The meaning behind dividing $Zi - Mi$ by $Fi - Mi$ was to express Ii in terms of the relative size of $Fi - Mi$ as a unit; so by this division Ii becomes a standardized measurement. Obviously, when $Zi = Mi$ the value of Ii will be zero, and when $Zi = Fi$ the value will be 1. In actual practice I will multiply this by 100, and when the current quantity of the welfare component exceeds 100, I will take it to mean that the F point has been reached.

The next equation expresses the total quantity of welfare, W.

$$W = a_1 I_1 + a_2 I_2 + \ldots + a_n I_n$$

176

$$= \sum_{i=1}^{n} a_i \, I_i = \sum_{i=1}^{n} a_i \, \frac{Z_i - M_i}{F_i - M_i}$$

Here $a_1, \ldots, a_n$ are the weights given to the components and 'n' is the number of components. In actual practice this W will be multiplied by $100/nk$, and similar to the case of the individual components, the M point is zero and the F point is 100 (k is a constant for coordination of the relative weights of the components).

The first equation is suggested from J. Drewnowski, *Studies in the Measurement of Levels of Living and Welfare,* (Geneva: U.N. Research Institute for Social Development Report no. 70/3 (Geneva: U.N. Research Institute for Social Development, 1970); but the method used to determine the M and F points is different.

The second equation needs some comments. In the first place, the summation of this formula is not the sum of different individuals but that of the various items. In the second place, there must be an assumption underlying the operation of the summation of items. That is that every item is mutually substitutable in the sense that these items are on the unidimensional continuum from the point of view of welfare. In the third place, the nature of our approach is not that of "maximization." The idea of the M and F points clearly demonstrates that the goal is not to maximize welfare, but to attain "civil minimum" or "civil standard."

9. This research project was done by four people under my leadership. It is reported in Ken'ichi Tominaga, Atsushi Naoi, Kazuo Seiyama and Bunshirō Ando, *Nikijunten hōshiki ni yoru fukushi shihyō sakusei no kokoromi* [An attempt to construct an indicator of social welfare in terms of a two-point standard] (Tokyo: Bureau of General Planning and Coordination, 1972. Also, Kazuo Seiyama, "Kōdo keizai seichō to seikatsu no shitsu" [High rates of economic growth and the quality of life] in Akuto Hiroshi, *et al.*, eds.

Hendōki no Nihon shakai [Japanese society at a point of change],(Tokyo: Nihon Hoso Shuppan Kyokai, 1972), 131-57.

10. The outline of the weighting method we used includes the following steps: (1) corresponding to each cell of Table 7-3 we selected one to three representative items, totaling forty-five; (2) each item was printed on a card; (3) respondents (1,000 random samples of Tokyo citizens) were asked through personal interview to sort these forty-five cards into five ranking categories: "very important," "somewhat important," "average," "somewhat unimportant," "unimportant"; (4) we calculated the mean scores of every cell by giving scores 100, 75, 50, 25, 0 respectively to the five categories above; and (5) we transformed the scores so that the grand mean equalled unity. The resulting final scores were used as the weights of the respective cells.

11. Professor Bell himself has to some extent admitted this point. Daniel Bell, "The Post-Industrial Society: the Evolution of an Idea," *Survey* (Spring 1971): 102-168, esp. 161.

12. It seems hardly accidental that Professor Bell acted as chairman of the "Panel on Social Indicator" in preparing the "Social Report" of the U.S. Department of Health, Education, and Welfare.

13. Ken'ichi Tominaga, "Sangyōka to shokugyō kōzō no hendō" [Industrialization and changes in the occupational structure] in *Sangyō shakai no dōtai*, Ch. V.

14. In this regard see the "National Preference Survey" of the Japanese Economic Planning Agency in which I participated in the planning and analysis: Keizai Kikakuchō *Nihonjin no manzokudo* [The Degree of Satisfaction of the Japanese People].

Part V
Information

Chapter Eight

New Trends
in the Media
of Japan

Yoshimi Uchikawa

While Japan has not yet become an "informational society" to the extent that information and knowledge replaced goods and energy as the nexus of the social and technological system, it is clearly experiencing a change in its communications of such proportion as to warrant recognition as a communication revolution.

This change is characterized, first of all, by a vast expansion in the communications media. Two examples taken from the mass media typify the change. First, the number of daily newspapers in 1971 belonging to the Japan Newspaper Publishers and Editors Association stood at eighty-eight, with a total circulation of 54,340,000 copies.[1] The diffusion of these daily newspapers has reached 0.51 copy per person. In addition, there are other dailies that are not the members of the association. No reliable statistics are available for them, but they include more than seventy small daily community papers and a number of free weekly shopping papers, which are proliferating in residential areas of large metropolitan centers.

Secondly, broadcasting, which in Japan is partly public

and partly private, also has greatly expanded. Public broadcasting is conducted by the Japan Broadcasting Corporation (NHK) while private broadcasting is done by a number of commercial corporations. In 1971, NHK broadcast prorams on its two networks, one general and the other educational, through 1,491 television stations, including relay stations.[2] The NHK also had 173 medium-wave radio stations, which broadcast programs on the basis of two similar networks (Radio 1 and Radio 2). In addition, Japan's public broadcasting had a total of 363 FM radio stations. In the private sector, in the same year there were 88 commercial broadcasting companies with 1,412 television stations. In addition, 52 commercial radio companies operated 161 medium-wave radio stations and 4 FM stations.[3] Although the government does not officially permit a network operation for commercial broadcasters, there exist *de facto* four private television networks on a nationwide basis.

This vast increase in broadcasting facilities was paralleled by an increase in the number of consumers. The number of television subscribers as of 1971 totaled 23,520,000 households: 84.4 percent of all Japanese households having black and white, and 42.3 percent having color television sets.[4]

The size of the media in Japan is the result of explosive growth over the past few years. The Economic Planning Agency reports that between 1955 and 1971, the circulation of daily newspapers per capita increased by 40 percent, the annual distribution of books per capita, by nearly 350 percent, the annual distribution of magazines per capita by more than 500 percent, and the number of television sets per hundred households by more than 750 percent (see Table 8-1).

In contrast, movie audences have been declining sharply ever since 1958. By 1971 the average Japanese was attending a movie theater only twice a year.

Personal communication by common carrier also has expanded. Ordinary mail service in 1970 rose by 1.69 times

Table 8-1
Diffusion of Mass Media

	TV (per 100 households)		Radio (per 100 h.s.)	Newspaper (a day per capita)	Book (a year per capita)	Magazine (a year per capita)
	Mono-chrome	Color				
1955	(10.4)[a]	—	73.8	0.37	1.1	3.0
1960	44.7	—	85.0 16.5	0.38	1.3	9.0
1965	90.0	—	70.3[b] 44.4[c]	0.44	2.2	9.8
1970	90.2	26.3	71.1	0.51	3.2	14.3
1971	84.4	42.3	69.8	0.51	4.9	18.5

[a] 1958
[b] Ordinary sets
[c] Transistor radios

Source: Keizai Kikakuchō, *Kokumin seikatsu hakusho* [White Paper on the National Livelihood, 1972] (Tokyo: Ōkurashō Insatsukyoku, 1972), p. 160.

over 1960 with a total of 11,485,800,000 items having been delivered.[5] Telephone service made an even more spectacular increase: in 1970 a total of 23,013,000 telephones were registered, representing twice as many as in 1965.[6]

Computers also are coming into more and more use. In fact it is the computer that has brought about the technological revolution in communications. At the end of March 1971, Japan had 9,482 computers (excluding mini computers costing less than $30,000), a number second only to those in use in the United States.[7]

Finally, data-processing companies, think-tanks and other business ventures that may be collectively termed the "information industry" have come to the fore. In fact, data communication systems are now being used by various banks, the Japanese Railway Corporation, and other firms. The Japan Telephone and Telegraph Corporation has set up a data communication service using the push-button telephone. The mass media also are using computers for management control and production processing.

Celebrating the fact that the informational revolution has begun and that Japan has entered the computer age, the Ministry of International Trade and Industry recently set aside the first week of October as "Informationalization Week." The first observance took place in 1972 with ceremonies and exhibitions in major cities throughout the country.

One result of this extraordinary diffusion of media is an impressive increase in the flow of information in Japanese society. Recently an attempt was made to quantify this trend. Defining the flow of information as "the significant movement of information from one place to another," data provided by the information-flow census of the postal ministry was studied to measure the number of bits of information that passed through some thirty different channels or media over the past fifteen years.[8] According to this study, the information supply in 1970 amounted to $2,572 \times 10^{16}$ bits. With an average annual growth of 12.2 percent, this represented an increase of 3.2 times over the past ten years. Nor is the end in sight. According to a recent study of the Comprehensive Research Institute of Telecommunications, the volume of information in Japan provided by eight different communications media may be expected by 1975 to be 1.61 times greater than in 1968, with the flow via television more than tripling in quantity (see Table 8-2).

Japan does indeed face an explosion of the dissemination of information. But how much of this information do the people take in? For example, how many of the $2,572 \times 10^{16}$ bits of information supplied in 1970 were actually accepted by the consuming public? Apparently only a fraction—an estimated 304×10^{16}. This did indeed represent a growth of 1.4 times over the consumption in 1960, but even so, consumers seem to have taken in only one-eighth of the information dispensed. It would appear then that the bulk of available information is wasted, confirming the experience of most householders that much of the mail sent to the home goes directly into the waste basket.

Table 8-2
Some Indicators of Estimated Volume of Information in 1975

	Volume in 1968 = 100
Expenses for research	180.4
Advertising	159.0
Distance of movement (per capita)	140.0
Frequency of use of means of transportation	134.3
Telephone	161.0
Letters	123.9
Television	304.4
Radio	143.5
Magazines	133.6
Books	166.7
Newspapers	122.2
Coefficient of information	160.7

Source: Denki Tsūshin Sōgō Kenkyūto *Role of Telecommunications in the Post-Industrial Society,* (Tokyo: Denki Tsūshin Sōgō Kenkyūto, 1970), p. 47.

There is, after all, a limit to the amount of information the human being can handle. The total consumption of information in 1970 of 304 x 10^{16} bits represents a daily per capita consumption of about 74 million bits, which is equivalent to the output of thirteen and a half hours of programs broadcast on black and white television. Thus, while the supply of information may be almost infinitely expandable, the absolute volume one can possibly consume is limited.

Does this growing excess of supply over individual consumption capacity mean that we are supplying too much information? The answer would seem to be affirmative if every individual needed exactly the same information; but in our contemporary free society each individual has different informational needs and desires. A capacity to disseminate excess information is necessary to permit freedom of choice as to what information one wants to receive. Also how well informational needs and desires are met depend upon the quality and variety of available information.

It is important to analyze, therefore, the changing quality and content of today's information. Such qualitative change as is taking place is of course a reflection of the changing needs for information on the part of the people who consume it.

Basically, these changed social needs reflect the change in social values occasioned by swift economic growth and the resultant improvement of the living standard. Up until World War II, Japanese values were based on Confucian morality and the concept of a family-state, whereby the emperor was not only the head of the state but also the father of that family to which all Japanese belonged. Thus the individual family was considered a fragment of the state, so that, in general, the Japanese found their highest value in the state.

As a result of Japan's defeat, the family-state concept collapsed and the value system of the Japanese people also disintegrated. Confronted as well with economic hardship, many Japanese began to think only of how they as "individuals'' could make money, improve their material lot, and live in peace. Now, with the dramatic economic prosperity of recent decades, other values are coming to the fore. In a survey of youth (18-22 years of age) conducted in the Tokyo-Yokohama area, in February 1971 by NHK's Institute of Broadcasting Culture, it was found that 84 percent were still primarily interested in things close to themselves, but not primarily of a material character (see Table 8-3).

Thus it would seem that with affluence has come a new set of nonphysiological needs, characterized by A. H. Maslow as strong desires for safety, belongingness, esteem, and self-actualization.[9] This pattern is found not only among the younger generation, but also among the elder generation. It represents a general pattern of changing needs on the part of modern Japanese.

In turn, these changing needs and outlook have changed the basic informational requirements. First of all, the need for diverse and extensive information has increased. Second, the intensified emphasis on the family and personal life has increased the demand for information relating to personal livelihood. Information for the enjoyment of leisure is

Table 8-3
"What Is the Goal of Your Life?"

	(% of Total)
To have a happy family	30
To engage in creative work	15
To run my own business	14
To devote myself to my profession	12
To live an ordinary life	11
To live as I please	5
To reform society	3
To devote myself to social service	2
To become rich	2
To attain high status	1
To do nothing in particular	1

Source: Daiji Kazama, "Gendai sein en ni miru ishiki to kōdō no genkyo" [Present State of Consciousness and Behavior of the Younger Generation], NHK Bunken Geppō (June 1972), p. 8.

of course part of it. Third, there has been a marked increase in the need for differentiated information for particular individuals or groups rather than for general information for the mass of society. And finally, there has been an increasing demand for information with an emotional rather than a rational appeal, and for the media that can transmit such information most effectively.

These new needs are affecting not only the quantity and quality of the information being made available, but the technology of communication as well. An interesting example is community antenna television (CATV). CATV was inaugurated in Japan in 1955, two years after the advent of television broadcasting, for the purpose of improving television reception in mountain districts. Although 70 percent of Japan's land area is mountainous, CATV has grown slowly. By April 1972, 9,300 communities had CATV facilities. The total number of subscribing homes had reached 900,000, with the usual facility serving only a very small community.[10]

But a new step forward was taken in 1968 with the establishment of the Tokyo Cablevision Network Company (TCN) at a terminal district in Tokyo. The TCN attracted attention for two reasons: it was the first CATV to improve poor reception of television in the city where conditions were aggravated by high-rise buildings and elevated speedways, and it was the first facility of its kind to operate as a business concern for profit.

From the beginning, Japan's CATV was engaged for the most part in relaying signals so as to enable a local area to receive television programs clearly. In the past few years, moreover, some of these CATV stations have begun to originate programs of their own as well, and efforts are now being made to disseminate such remotely-produced programs more widely. The resulting increase in the available number of programs has been very well received by subscribers.

The real potential of CATV as a new communications

medium lies in the future of coaxial cable. In anticipation of this, the postal ministry founded the Research Council of the Coaxial Cable Information System (CCIS) to study possible regulations, economic and technical problems. In fact the postal ministry and the Tokyo metropolitan government are jointly intending to build a wired city by means of coaxial cable at Tama New Town, a suburb of Tokyo.

Excitement has been generated by the advent of coaxial cable because such a television communication system will not be restricted by governmental frequency allocations, but will be free to utilize many different channels in order to meet diversified demands. Moreover, two-way communication will be technically possible. Coaxial cable, therefore, may serve to integrate small residential groups which have been disrupted by rapid changes in their living patterns and thus help them develop a more satisfying sense of community.

Another new device, the video package, is already on the market. It is a video tape which can be bought and played in one's own television set at one's own convenience. With obvious utility for teaching as well as for greater leisure enjoyment, such packages are being offered in the United States as Electronic Video Recording by the Columbia Broadcasting System and Selecta Vision by the Radio Corporation of America. In 1969, Japan Victor and Sony successively put on the market their versions, consisting of a cassette for color video tape recording and a playback unit. Other companies as well are now active.

The fact that each of these devices is an extension of television underlines the fact that television is at the center of the informational revolution. According to the postal ministry's study cited earlier, already in 1960 television was providing 57.7 percent of the information being disseminated in Japan. By 1970 its share had risen to 88.6 percent.

On the other hand, in the same year television's share in the total volume of information consumed was only 41 percent. The printed media obviously remain important. Nevertheless, according to a recent survey by NHK of the

189

time each day the Japanese allocate to the various media, the average citizen spends an extraordinary amount of his day watching television—as much as three hours by 1970 (see Table 8-4).

One interesting result of this survey is that while the time devoted to television gained rapidly in the early sixties, it is now leveling off. This data is corroborated by other polls which show that there has in fact been a decline in popular interest in television over the last five years (see Table 8-5). The explanation may be that the Japanese people are now becoming so accustomed to television that they are becoming more selective in what they watch. This is the challenge to commercial television in the future, and one to which CATV is likely to help it respond.

As indicated above, newspapers continue to hold their own in the citizens' attention, with affluence increasing the desire of individuals to hold their own copies. As a result, newspaper circulation in Japan has risen steadily since the end of World War II. This trend has not changed in the past decade, the aggregate growth in circulation between 1961 and 1971 being 17 million copies. Also, newspapers still lead in advertising revenues, registering 34.1 percent of the market in 1971 as against 33 percent for commercial television.[11]

Like the other media, the press in recent years has been experiencing extensive technological innovation. In 1959, the *Asahi Shinbun* led the world by beginning to send its entire newspaper, by facsimile, a distance of 1,000 kilometers from Tokyo to Sapporo, Hokkaido, where it was printed by offset for local distribution. By March 1971, eleven Japanese newspapers had replaced their old Chinese-character teletype with similar transmission to thirteen cities.

A second technical innovation is the adaptation of the photocomposing machine in combination with offset—the so-called cold type system. Full-scale cold-type production in a daily newspaper was first adopted by the *Saga Shinbun* in 1969, but from 1971 and 1972 cold-type was being utilized

190

Table 8-4
Time Spent per Day by Japanese on Various Media

	(In minutes)		
	1960	*1965*	*1970*
Television	56	172	185
Print	29	31	30

Source: Fumiya Ogawa, "Informationalized Society and the Function of Television," Denpa Jihō (September 1972), p. 7.

Table 8-5
Changing Popular Interest in Television

	1967	*1971*
More interested than before	35%	25%
Interest the same as before	38	37
Less interested than before	11	19
Not interested before and still not	8	14

Source: "Informationalized Society," p. 9.

by such gigantic newspapers as *Nihon Keizai Shinbun* and *Asahi Shinbun*.

Computerization is a third extensive innovation introduced by the Japanese press. As of 1971, eighteen newspaper companies had thirty-three computers. Of these, nine companies were using thirteen units in production. *Asahi Shinbun* plans to automate the whole process of editing, layout and printing of the newspaper by joining cold-type system devices with the computer.

Another promising technological development is the Home Facsimile Newspaper. More than 90 percent of all daily newspapers published in Japan are delivered to the subscriber's home every morning and every evening. But increasing traffic congestion, rising labor cost and other factors are posing problems for this delivery system. If it were possible to receive a newspaper in the home by means of facsimile, the process of printing as well as the cost and time needed for the delivery could be eliminated. Such a newspaper would have the added advantage of securing the instantaneousness that so far only the electronic media can claim, while preserving its own intrinsic characteristic of recordability.

The first attempt to utilize facsimile transmission techniques for sending a newspaper electronically to the home was made by the *Mainichi Shinbun* in 1964. But the home facsimile newspaper truly attracted the public's attention only in September 1969, when Matsushita Electric Industries and the Toshiba Electric Company simultaneously announced their respective systems for this purpose. Matsushita proposed to use the redundant television spectrum for transmission and to attach an adaptor to the ordinary TV set for reception. The Toshiba system utilized electric waves and required a special receiving device. Experimentation continues, but the obstacles are real. So far, the cost of both the receiver or adaptor and the recording paper are prohibitive. In addition, doubts are arising about the urgency of the public's needs for such a service. It seems more likely now that the potential market may be limited for the time being to specialized individuals, firms, stores, and schools.

Newspapers are changing in other ways as well, particularly under the impact of television. Some people feel that the newspaper had to surrender its function of first reporting to television and instead had to move to secondary, that is, analytical and interpretive, reporting. It is true that more people today get the news first by television. On the other hand, a growing number of people rely on the written press to confirm the news they first learn on the screen. Moreover, most people still look to the press for the essential news of politics, international affairs, economics, society, science, and culture. Only the newspaper is capable of providing such vital information in a compact and inexpensive manner, and of putting it in an order of importance. In these circumstances it is certain that the press will continue to play a leading role among the information media.

Furthermore, the traditional role of the written press as the watchdog of society, for example, on the current matter of pollution, is becoming even more important than before. How to perform this function effectively is one of the Japanese press's greatest challenges.

Another challenge is the recent rise of "miniature" communication media known in Japan as the *mini-komi*. These characteristically take the form of tiny newspapers, mostly mimeographed, which are circulated among groups of young people or within specific residential communities; some are overt, others are underground. No doubt a response to the new inclination of the people to seek information to suit their own needs and to participate in society more fully by expressing their own views, the growing *mini-komi* are challenging the regular press to offer a more varied service than ever before if it is to meet effectively the needs of the new age.

Clearly Japanese society is being overwhelmed by information and will be even more so as the technology of communication improves. Unfortunately, most of this information is commercial and entertaining, obscuring the information of enduring value in a maelstrom of the misleading and the ephemeral. How to help the receiver select the information he truly needs out of the data he is offered is an important task for us in the future.

Notes

1. Nihon Shinbun Kyōkai, *Nihon shinbun nenkan, 1972* [Japanese Newspaper Annual 1972] (Tokyo: Dentsu, 1972), pp. 531-32.

2. Nihon Hōsō Kyōkai, *Nihon hōsō shuppan kyokai, 1972* [Radio and Television Yearbook, 1972], pp. 594, 599.

3. Ibid., pp. 608-619.

4. Ibid., p. 517.

5. Asahi Shinbunsha, *Asahi nenkan, 1972* (Tokyo: Asahi Shinbunsha, 1972), p. 510.

6. Ibid., p. 510.

7. Ibid., p. 501.

8. Mamoru Hashiguchi, "Jōhō ryūtsū ryō no jittai" [Actual state of the volume of the flow of information], *Nihon Keizai Shinbun,* May 4, 1972.

9. A.M. Maslow, *Motivation and Personality* (New York: Harper and Row, 1954).

10. Katsumi Soyama, "Possibility of CCIS and Informationalization," *Denpa Jihō,* June, 1972, p. 19.

11. Dentsū, *Dentsū kōkoku nenkan, 1972* [Dentsū advertising annual, 1972] (Tokyo: Dentsū, 1972), p. 273.

Chapter Nine

Information and Communication in the Not-So-New Society

Charles Frankel

A multitude of causes, unknown to former times, are now acting with a combined force to blunt the discriminating powers of the mind, and, unfitting it for all voluntary exertion, to reduce it to a state of almost savage torpor. The most effective of these causes are the great national events which are daily taking place, and the increasing accumulation of men in cities, where the uniformity of their occupations produces a craving for extraordinary incident which the rapid communication of intelligence hourly gratifies. To this tendency of life and manners the literature and theatrical exhibitions of the country have conformed themselves. The invaluable works of our elder writers, I had almost said the works of Shakespeare and Milton, are driven into neglect by frantic novels, sickly and stupid German Tragedies, and deluges of idle and extravagant stories in verse.[1]

So wrote Wordsworth in 1805 about the condition of human communication in his time. It may suggest a useful moral for our own inquiry: our age is not in every respect as unique as it flatters or berates itself for being. Indeed, it may be that what marks this age off from other ages is precisely the dissolution or foreshortening of its sense of historic time, its distinctive incapacity to believe in its continuity with other ages.

I do not doubt that something profound is taking place in our societies, and that its source lies in the rapid acquisition and dissemination of information. I shall try later on to indicate in what ways this new historic current, at once technological and psychological, managerial and moral, may be bringing about a significant alteration in the characteristics of human experience. But what is taking place, I believe, is less the result of a sudden mutation than of an evolutionary process that has long been at work. It is the acceleration of trends that began to take powerful shape, in the Occident, and I think in Japan as well, at least 200 years ago. Indeed, in some ways we are dealing with phenomena which are as old as large cities—and this makes them 2,500 years old and older. There are complaints, it will be recalled, in the pages of Thucydides and Plato about the distressing characteristics of thought and opinion in crowded, sensation-seeking, egalitarian-minded societies.

It might be best to begin, then, by noting what the present "information revolution" and "knowledge explosion" are *not*. We can then go on more safely to speak of their distinctive positive characteristics.

I would begin with a matter of vocabulary. If the word *information* is taken in its strictest meaning, to signify "the communication of intelligence," or "instruction,"[2] it is not the right word to use as a general descriptive label for what is taking place today in advanced industrial societies like Japan and the United States. A more accurate, less tendentious word would be *communication*.

Undoubtedly, the flow of communications today is more intense than ever before and affects more people. Undoubtedly, too, these communications travel across greater distances, make the rounds incomparably more speedily, and introduce into the individual's consciousness an awareness and concern about events whose physical remoteness from him is, by the standards of earlier societies, immense. Individuals in many places, furthermore, are reached by communications a significant proportion of which are uniform in content and form. Walter Cronkite is a personage in Washington and Dubuque, California and Mississippi. The uniformity, indeed, crosses national boundaries. There is unprecedented similarity in many of the communications reaching Japanese and Americans, for the great metropolitan centers of communication have become international in their interests and reach, and cater to audiences around the world. Terrorism in Belfast or Munich; racial tensions in New York or London; war and peace in Vietnam; the advantages of Sony transistors and American prefabs; blue jeans, rock music, student demonstrations; the films of Truffaut and Bergmann; the novels of Solzhenitsyn or Gunter Grass; the analysis of events in *Time* or the *American Journal of Sociology*—Americans and Japanese alike respond to all of these, although they do not necessarily respond in the same way.

But when we consider the range and variety of this traffic, the word *information* is obviously inadequate to describe it. Flat misinformation is surely as plentiful as accurate intelligence. And much is pure speculation, and much else is impure speculation or sheer noise. Nor are we dealing mainly with cognitive or even pseudocognitive materials: to most of what is communicated the words *true, false, speculative,* and even *nonsense* do not apply. What beats upon, or insinuates itself into, the individual cerebrum is fantasy, invective, prayer, inspiration, consolation, entertainment, temptation, reassurance, and so forth. Of course, the proposition is true that more certifiable "knowledge" is also pumped into the channels of mass communication today than in any previous era. Even in totalitarian societies, there is incomparably more reliable information—for example, on the dietary needs of children—available to citizens. But the significance of this communication of new knowledge must be measured not simply against the standard of the past, but in terms of its relation to the total *present* communications traffic. The great proportion of this traffic has little or nothing to do with knowledge, and much more to do with the "savage torpor" and "craving for extraordinary incident" which worried Wordsworth.

Even when we restrict our attention to the communication of what has a claim to the label of "knowledge" or would-be "knowledge," there are strong grounds for caution in using such phrases as "the knowledge explosion." It goes without saying that in the present century, and certainly within the last thirty or forty years, there has been astonishing intellectual achievement, at once dazzling, inspiring, and disorienting. The human race, taken as a unit, possesses immeasurably more extensive knowledge about physics, chemistry, astronomy, or geology. In recent years, biology in particular has made impressive strides. Nevertheless, once this is said, there are qualifications that have to be added immediately.

First, despite prevalent assumptions to the contrary, we have no assurance that the phenomenal rate of discovery which has marked recent decades will continue, much less accelerate. The projection of current tendencies into the future may not be a mistake, but it is in part an act of faith. For while it is true that societies like Japan and the United States are organized to conduct "research and development" in systematic fashion, most of this "research and development" consists in finding new technical applications of basic scientific theories and discoveries. And the decisive factor affecting the pace of discovery is the tempo and character of developments in basic scientific theory.

These, however, are affected by a broad range of variables, almost all of which are subject to considerable vicissitudes. The accelerating pace of scientific discovery, far from being an inexorable fact of life, is dependent on conditions which are likely to be safe only if we go to considerable lengths to protect them. Among the factors on which progress in basic scientific theory depends are the following: the character and distribution of research facilities; the efficiency of supporting services (for example, availability of middle-level technicians, competence of suppliers and maintenance people, quality of library facilities and of information retrieval); the morale and cohesion of the scientific community (for example, its freedom to conduct its business without regard to questions of race or ideology, and independently of the political divisions in the external society); shifting motivations and prestige structures, affecting the choice of careers and the movement of talent; and the quality of education, particularly as it affects the recruiting, orienting, and training of elites.

Nor are these all. The prevailing cultural climate has always been a factor in the evolution of scientific inquiry, but it is probably more of a factor at present than in the past. Scientific endeavor could be sustained in the past with the support of a few powerful or wealthy patrons, coming down from their protected promontories to give their aid and comfort to Mineroc. This is increasingly difficult at present. Science is dependent on an expensive infrastructure, and this infrastructure, in its turn, is dependent on the willingness of legislatures and political authorities to allot the taxpayers' money to its support. That willingness, it has become evident, is not indefinitely expandable. It has still to be shown, indeed, that the reduction of international military and economic rivalries will not do harm to scientific progress by removing the principal reasons for which public support has been given.

In general, the rate of scientific progress in the future is likely to depend on the levels of tolerance that exist in the society at large for one or both of two things: social inequality, or expensive intellectual "irrelevance." On the whole, it is in societies where inequality has been accepted or enforced, or where splendid uselessness or even wastefulness has been admired—and the two conditions usually go together—that major achievements in the basic sciences have taken place. Tyrannies can maintain such conditions, though even they have difficulty doing so under contemporary conditions and are usually forced to obfuscate their purposes. As for democracies, it remains to be seen whether they are capable of this kind of tolerance, at any rate democracies in a more peaceful world. For nationalist competition has been a major factor in the support which democratic governments have so far given the sciences. [3]

And beyond these matters, there is simply the question of random chance. Assuming intellectual progress, *what* basic discoveries will be made? For not all discoveries are equally susceptible to mass dissemination or to practical technological exploitation. We cannot know in advance what scientific inquiry is likely to turn up. (If we did we would already know what we don't know, and the inquiry would be unnecessary.) And still less can we know in advance *who* is likely to be engaged in what branch of science, or in any science at all. Much depends on the luck of the genetic draw. The most fertile developments in science, those which open up previously unsuspected fields of inquiry, are usually radically discontinuous from what precedes them, and are the work of idiosyncratic geniuses whose appearance in history represents a fortuitous concurrence of rare aptitudes with a suitable environment and opportunity.

Indeed, with respect to the present moment and the evolving future, it would be useful to reflect on the fact that, for the past generation, natural science has been living principally on the remarkable intellectual capital created for it by men such as Einstein, Bohr, Heisenberg, Mendel, Von Neumann, and a few others. All these men, as well as their peers in other fields of inquiry—for example, Freud, Weber, Keynes, Bertrand Russell—were the products of the pre-World War I European culture, now irrecoverable. I find this a sobering thought.

I find it all the more sobering when I reflect on the pressures under which universities, which emerged in the present century as the distinctive polities for nurturing an independent intellectual culture, are currently laboring. Their basic difficulties are not due to phenomena which we may take to be evanescent, like the Indochina war. In my opinion, they are due, first, to the growing pressure to homogenize all institutions of higher education, to make them all symbols of the national commitment to equality, and, second, to the rise and spread of a new culture and ethic which deprecate rigorous intellectual effort and which regard it as a mark of effete snobbism and elitism. Needless to say, Left and Right seem in agreement on this point, as they are so often in agreement on others. And while these phenomena are conspicuous on the American scene, they are not peculiar to it.

I do not know whether universities as we have known them will manage to survive. Perhaps other institutions, equally serviceable for the maintenance of a scientific tradition and culture, will take their place. In any event, whatever happens, we cannot operate on the cheerful assumption that because modern societies now depend crucially on a steady supply of fruitful information, they will do the necessary things to maintain the institutions from which this supply comes. Nothing in the history of mankind, and certainly nothing in the history of the present generation, suggests that people can be counted on to do what is good for them. Very often, disaster is necessary to prompt them to act in their own self-interest; and, even then, they may very well treat as scapegoats the very institutions on which the solution of their problems depends. That is the recent history of universities.

On balance, to be sure, it is probably best to suppose that scientific achievement in the next thirty to fifty years will be as surprising and as pregnant with practical consequences as the achievements of the past generation. Of all the possibilities, this seems the most likely. Nevertheless, we must realize that predictions about "the information society" encompass much more than a reasoned guess about the future course of science. They rest as well on social, political, and genetic assumptions of considerable magnitude and some precariousness. Not only can we not assume that scientific progress is automatic, but we should be careful of the softer version of the old belief in the inevitability of intellectual progress which suggests that, short of political tyranny or nuclear catastrophe, scientific advance at the present tempo or better is just naturally in the cards. This treats science as though its history were more independent of cultural twists and turns than I believe it is.

A final word should also be said on a view which is close to the old notion of automatic "progress." It holds that scientific and technical developments are not merely the principal determinants of historical change but are bound to shape a culture that is congenial to them. Such an assumption is present in many futurological speculations, both optimistic and pessimistic, and in many of the discussions built on phrases like "the technetronic era." Needless to say, I do not wish to deny the immense social and cultural impact of science and technology. Nevertheless, these analyses and speculations seem to me in many ways closer to theology than empirical observation. They express, in disguised form, the classic religious desire for a rational plan of existence, and the classic religious unwillingness to believe that the world we inhabit is so constructed that accidental events and small causes, even foolish and idiotic ones, can have major consequences. Accordingly, they imagine a future that will be subject, above all, to the remorseless pressure of supremely rational factors like science and technology.

It may be that science and technology will successfully shape human culture in their image. Not only the assembly line and cost-benefit analyses, but the time table, the batting average, the efficiency apartment, the decline of the family and of marriage, are indications of how deeply they have already penetrated human thinking and behavior. But science and technology may also turn loose intense and violent reactions against themselves. Witness the romanticism and evangelicalism of the nineteenth century, or the present resurgence of ethnic and nationalistic outlooks, and of the *nostalgie de la boue*. And, of course, cultural developments may depend on more or less independent and unpredictable variables. Who in 1960, for example, looking at satellites and electronics, the theory of games, or the economies of Keynes, would have predicted the emergence of the Beatles, or the seismic effect they had on mass culture, youth and adult lifestyles and clothes-styles, and, very probably, on education and politics? They used technology, to be sure, to amplify their voices and chemistry to raise their spirits. But their style, the content of their message, and their success could not have been anticipated. Just as in the sciences, cultural evolution is the work, in some considerable measure, of unpredictable individuals.

A second qualification which should be borne in mind when phrases like "the knowledge explosion" are used is that there is legitimate ground for wondering whether the noises we have been hearing are everywhere explosions or only the bursting of paper bags. The remarkable growth in reliable knowledge which has marked the present century is pretty much limited, at any rate if we are talking about the discovery of laws and the formulation of confirmed theories, to the natural sciences.

A significant though partial exception to this generalization may perhaps be made for economics, although there are eminent economists whose competence to judge is better than mine, and who tell me I am wrong. And of course it can hardly be gainsaid that improved methods of sampling and statistical analysis, and more sophisticated techniques of interviewing and empirical observation, have provided us with great bodies of reliable information about social questions, from the incidence of infant mortality to the voting habits of the Boston Irish, not available a generation ago. On many subjects we have fairly precise factual information where speculation and rough generalization once ruled. However, these nuggets of reliable information are scattered. By and large, we lack explanatory frameworks for them which allow us to understand why they are as they are or what inferences and predictions it is reasonable to base upon them.

"Knowledge explosion?" The fact is that, with respect to most of the grievous issues that plague us, we do not know more than to strike out manfully in the dark. The equalization of educational opportunity; the elimination of racial segregation; the discouragement of violence and crime; the cure of drug addiction; the alienation of youth; reversing the decay of the inner cities; the solution of the problem of chronic poverty, or if not that, at least the economical and humane care of the chronically poor; even the simple, circumscribed problem of teaching reading, writing, and arithmetic more effectively: every one of these is a matter on which we have passionate assertion but only the most equivocal information. Even in economics the significance of such a major phenomenon of modern life as advertising is a subject of debate in which ideology plays a larger part than empirical information. Consider the following from one of the most respected economists: "It is by no means unlikely that advertising has significant net effects. . . . But at present we cannot say whether this is so or not, because, after a quarter-century during which advertising has become one of the outstanding features of our economic life, and scientific economics has been intensively developed, the relevant experiments have never been tried."[4]

The Victorians are belabored for the unenlightened and doctrinaire views on which they based their behavior. Looking back, we are stunned that, despite the disasters that befall them, they allowed experience to change their opinions only very slowly and with the greatest reluctance. In contrast the convention reigns that our society is one in which sound knowledge is available, in fact or potentially, for the solution of most or all serious social problems. We are allowing this convention to change only very slowly and with the greatest reluctance despite our own experiences with disappointment.

In sum, the so-called knowledge explosion is, in the human sciences, pretty much a publicist's dream. The illusion that we are better informed remains widespread, however, and this is a significant social fact. One of the repeated experiences, for example, in an official's life in Washington, particularly an official with an academic background, is the meeting at which congressional leaders, distinguished citizens, or presidential advisers, confronted by a problem, will say hopefully, will insist almost pugnaciously, that "the scientists, the people who study these things," must have worked out some kind of answer to them, and then turn to him challengingly to find the people and come up with that answer. And the official will find, if he takes the trouble to look, that there are always "scientists, people who study these things," who do not think it right to disappoint such a noble hope. In this sense the outlines of a new ethic, appropriate to an "information society," can be clearly discerned. Whether this is to be welcomed or not I leave to others to say.

Having given these cautionary doubts their due, let me now indicate some of the reasons I believe that labels such as "the information society" or "postindustrial society" can properly be used to describe the state of affairs in communication that currently exists or is emerging.

There is, first of all, the phenomenon of *amplification*. Given the instrumentalities of communication perfected over the last quarter of a century, more people, both in absolute numbers and in terms of relative proportions of all populations, are reached by the communications originated, authorized, or permitted by those in key positions in the great communication centers. The voices of those who have access to these media are amplified; the powers of hearing of almost all of us are also amplified: we hear more, and from a greater distance from the communication's point of origin.

Some of the more obvious consequences are plain. On the one side, control of centralized media of communication is obviously a new political instrument of enormous power, and monopolistic control of such media makes possible forms of tyranny more complete than most of those known in the past. On the other side, the problem-solving resources potentially available to individuals have been exponentially increased. Information on disease, economic opportunities, educational programs, social assistance facilities, the extermination of pests—an indefinite list—is all there more or less for the asking. Information—retrieval systems make it incomparably easier to find the information the individual needs; radio, television, films, the Sunday newspaper, immensely increase the power of the society to break into the individual's social or cultural enclave and convey useful information to him that he doesn't know he needs until he has it.

But there are other consequences as well, and the accumulation of these consequences is also part of what we mean when we use phrases like "postindustrial society" and try to communicate by them the notion that human experience in countries like Japan and the United States is changing profoundly. Among all of these I would dwell on what is perhaps most notable: the widespread sense of frustration induced by the existence of powerful media of communication. There is no reason to think that there is more tragedy per capita in the world today than in previous times. In all probability, there is less. But there are more people, and so quantitatively there is more trouble; and incomparably more of this trouble is reported, recorded, diagnosed, prayed over, deplored; and, thanks to the mass media of communication, very much larger numbers of people, often at considerable distances, are apprised of these events. But those in a position to do anything about the tragedies reported—the wars, terrors, tyrannies, famines, slaughters, earthquakes, crashes, wrecks, hijackings, persecutions, brigandages, insults, humiliations, lies, and consuming human wretchedness—are, in each individual case, only a small proportion of this audience. In sum, the communicated world outruns the world as a theater of individual action.

We are like the spectators in a theater looking on ghastly

events enacted on the stage before us, and then told—as the media do tell us, and as democratic ideology also leads us to suppose—that it is *we* who are responsible, and *we* who must do something about it. And yet we are not offered any effective way of getting up on the stage and contributing to the action except on rare occasions. Even powerful and influential people are helpless spectators with respect to the overwhelming proportion of the events that intrude on their consciousness—much more so, probably, than the powerful in the past, whose field of conscious awareness was not likely to outrun so greatly the field of their possible effective performance. As in other fields, so in communication as well: the growth of contemporary man's technical powers has helped to produce his aggravated sense of powerlessness. Perhaps it is against this background—the background of the daily diet of frustration on which the individual, caught between the communicated world and his personal, active world, must live—that the recurrent outbreaks of mass violence that mark the behavior of the supposedly routinized and subdued populations of postindustrial societies can better be understood.

Let us now turn to other new issues provoked by changes in information and communication. In international relations some particularly significant issues arise, particularly in regard to moral and social values.

"The knowledge explosion" has been greatest in the natural sciences, and the systematic application of new knowledge to the social system is easiest when the purpose of doing so is (or seems to be) simple, clear, and urgent, when the human beings directly involved can be closely and successfully controlled, and when their motives for continuing cooperation are strong. By and large, this means that the domain of military policy, planning, and practice is frequently the first to feel the large-scale impact of technological innovations and to attempt to use new scientific advances (for example, theory of games, operant-conditioning in psychology, programmed learning, and so forth) to alter exisiting structures and habits. The changes in military technology during the last thirty years have already produced a state of affairs which may be described as "the severance of war from politics." Assuming that nothing happens on the international military scene in the future but the very modest forms of disarmament envisaged in the SALT agreements, this state of affairs can be expected to persist and grow.

By "the severance of war from politics" I do *not* mean, of course, that wars, if they should come, will not have political causes. I mean that war between major powers, which, even in World War II, could be envisaged as a reasonable, albeit ghastly and costly, instrument for achieving or protecting certain fundamental political interests, can no longer be so viewed by sane men. The old maxim no longer holds: so far as the nuclear powers are concerned, war (that is, nuclear war, or any other major confrontation that runs the risk of escalation) is no longer the continuance of politics by other means. There is *no* rational political purpose, however selfish, that can be served by nuclear war. This means that the utility of nuclear weapons as chips in diplomacy is also nullified. Expensive and dangerous though nuclear armaments are, the great powers cannot use the threat of nuclear war as an effective means for advancing any national purpose except that of deterring others from a use of nuclear power.

I shall not discuss the impact of this state of affairs on the traditional conduct of international diplomacy, which would take us far afield. But while the dangers of a worldwide conflagration have probably been reduced, the persistence of this state of affairs is nevertheless likely to be a source of major strain in societies of the future. To the extent that the governments of the United States and the USSR (and China and Japan, if they enter the list in full competition) maintain a nuclear capability at, or anywhere near, present levels of expensiveness and destructiveness, they will, I believe, continue to tend to undermine their legitimacy in the eyes of their own citizens, and to maintain an international climate in which cynicism and frustration mount, and the resort by disgruntled groups and small nations to acts of violence and terror will always have a kind of ready-made defense. Perhaps most to the point of our present symposium, if the large nations continue to find no better way to maintain peace than by the balance of terror, the contribution of these governments to the demoralization (in the literal sense of the word) of the peoples of the world will continue to be immense. There are many efforts to explain why "authority" is in decline, why "human values" are flouted and ignored, why sadism has become a cult, why irrationalism is advertised as the cure of the world's woes. No doubt there are some profound reasons, not yet fully understood, for these endemic disorders of our "information-oriented" society. But is there any doubt, really, that some of the causes are quite apparent, and that a principal one is the highly visible, and highly rationalized (planned, systematized, and excused) irrationality of military and foreign policy?

Indeed, apart from nuclear war, the new technology has created conditions which reverse the circumstances in which wars were fought a century ago, and which also, in their way, illustrate "the severance of war from politics." To be sure, the United States has shown in the past year that the new technology available for "conventional" warfare makes it possible to direct an unprecedented amount of destructive power against an unprotected enemy while exposing only a very small number of professional airmen to the dangers of combat. This has not provided evidence that a war can be fought successfully in this manner. But it does show that a government can, in this way, remove a war from the mainstream of its own nation's daily experience, and successfully defuse it as a political issue. At any rate, it shows that an American government can perform this miracle at least once. Nevertheless, it seems to me unlikely that such an exercise will be repeated by the United States or by other governments that have witnessed the risks and the cost. On the whole, though technology makes such a war possible, it also makes it exceptionally difficult to sustain for an extended period of time: the bombers drop big payloads, but the television sets let people see what is happening, and the communications media bring back the reactions, which are instantaneous, massive, worldwide, and capable of more than blunting the psychological impact of technological terror on the enemy. The large nation that uses such means against a small nation is almost always the loser in worldwide political terms.

This remark leads to another: there has been a second major change in the character and conditions of international relations—the rise of the intellectuals and the professional communicators to positions of growing influence over the evolution of events. A number of factors explains this phenomenon: one is the secularization of society, and the key position occupied, in consequence, by secular intellectuals as the "censor class," the people whose judgments on the quality and moral condition of their society tend, over the long run, to receive the most sustained attention; another is the steadily higher proportions of the population exposed to higher education, and therefore to the culture of the intellectuals; still another is the prestige, justified or not, of men of learning in an "information era"; and, last but not least, there is the technology of communications, which makes intellectual enterprise, or, at any rate, intellectual celebrities, more visible, and which converts archetypical intellectuals—for example Jean-Paul Sartre, Yukio Mishima, Linus Pauling—into eminences of worldwide importance.

It is not plain in what direction, if any, the influence on international affairs of this newly powerful social category will be exerted. On the one side, the intellectuals and communicators who come from established and rich countries show themselves increasingly indifferent to, or impatient with, the restrictions imposed by national sovereignties and frontiers. On the other side, along with their confreres in the new countries, they have shown themselves, to a considerable extent, to be the creatures, indeed the articulators, of the ideologies and war cries that at once inflame and darken the international scene. But it seems probable that no nation will be able to sustain a foreign policy for an extended period without obtaining the assent, or at least the silence, of this key social group. In the richer nations this means that policies with a large military ingredient will create internal tensions dangerous to the stability of government, and inviting measures, mild or extreme, to put the intellectuals in their place. Once again, the price that is paid for this is the diminishment of the regime's moral authority, and, in daily life, the moral disorientation and discouragement of ordinary people, perhaps particularly the educated young.

I turn now to more intimate matters—the direct impact on individuals of life in an "information society." There has been much written on this subject, most of it tendentious, little of it supportable by unequivocal evidence. On the one hand, many complaints, whether about computers or mass communications, bespeak only a misplaced nostalgia for golden peasant days that never were; quite often, they express profoundly antidemocratic values as well. On the other hand, a good many of the hopes that are expressed for the educational value of the new communications seem to me to rest on nothing more substantial than the superstition that *any* technological invention must be good for us, else why would God have allowed us to invent it? Admittedly, the point is usually put somewhat more softly, but I think that is the essential message.

In the final analysis, generalizations about "the information society" are hazardous for the simple reason that so much depends on the content and quality of *what* is communicated, and on the content and quality of the brain that absorbs it. These are matters not entirely dependent on information and communications technologies. Despite the onslaughts that industrial society makes upon them, traits of

211

character and habits of mind and feeling whose roots are in traditional cultures have shown considerable powers of endurance. "Culture" is to some extent an autonomous realm, independent of economic and technological changes: men go on "living in the past," and the information system and mass communications are used to serve and reinforce such behavior: witness the cold war, Vietnam, the bombings in Belfast, the terror in the Middle East. Nor are these opinions wholly un-Marxist. Marx's complaint, if I understand him, was that culture (the "superstructure"), though it was materially determined, caught on to this fact slowly, and lagged behind the modes of production in its evolution: human beings, like the captives in Plato's cave, go on mistaking shadows for substantial realities.

However, despite these strong reservations, it is possible and useful to suggest a few generalizations about the impact of "the information society" on the daily experience of human beings. The new technologies do carry certain implications with regard to forms of human association; and these, in turn, carry implications for the organization of work, the character of leisure, and moral and social values. I shall be painfully selective in the discussion that follows, and I shall focus on *problems,* though I recognize that this is at the expense of leaving out some of the more positive potentialities of the new order of things.

Critics of industrial society have long discussed a tendency within it to a kind of deformed efficiency. Max Weber and Karl Mannheim used the distinction between "substantive" and "formal" rationality to describe it. John Dewey spoke of "the separation of means and ends," and of the split between "science" and "morals." Polanyi has described "the great transformation" of habits of thought and feeling involved in the separation of the capitalist market from the restrictions of traditional religious and ethical considerations. Gradually since the Middle Ages, and with greater and greater speed since the eighteenth century, modern civilization has learned to perform a kind of mental sleight-of-hand.

It defines certain issues as "neutral" and "technical," and deals with them with high intelligence, while at the same time assuming that the larger moral issues are essentially taking care of themselves.[5] This sleight-of-hand has brought great benefits, for example, in the expansion of productivity; the harm it has done is also great. What we have seen during the recent years—a war fought by Americans at a great distance from earth-level, and turned into an almost mechanical performance—is simply a grisly enactment of this institutionalized capacity of contemporary societies to put themselves at a distance from the moral significance of what they are doing.

In relation to the themes immediately under examination, this tendency takes the shape of "the severance of information from culture." In the absence of deliberate political, organizational, and educational safeguards, we may expect the aggravation of this tendency in "the information society." An information and communications technology, like any other technology, has certain characteristics. It is usually tailor-made to serve a predetermined end, and it exemplifies and reinforces a certain style of mind. That style is to narrow the frame of reference, and to seek to subordinate thought and action to a selected, identifiable, "hard" purpose. The definable benefit, the measurable gain in power and efficiency which a new technology brings, is generally taken to be a sufficiently persuasive case for adopting it. And since the consequences which it may bring are speculative and vague, and cannot be weighed in the balance with the explicitness that the technological mentality respects, they are dismissed as extraneous to the choices and judgments that have to be made. Thus great floods of information are efficiently organized, and remarkable ingenuity is employed, for example, for the purpose of improving automobile access to the cities. At the same time, little or nothing is done to examine or act against the physiological and emotional costs of the traffic jams this generates.

In an economy increasingly dependent on the formal

213

communication of information and counsel over long distances, the tendency to use information to advance predetermined purposes, without regard to side-effects, is likely
to become more pronounced. It might be said that the fault of
"the information society" is that it asks for, and receives,
too little information. The questions are prepackaged and
narrowly defined; the answers are programmed to these set
purposes. "Noise," static, disruption, become increasingly
necessary if the channels of intraorganizational communication are to be broken in upon with messages from the outside.
The inertia, the impersonal momentum of action, which
characterizes large organizations is one of the conspicuous
features of our societies. The thought that the growth in
influence of "the knowledge industry" will upset this
momentum is in part only a pious hope. The flow of "information" through channels, on the contrary, can serve simply
to reinforce and rationalize the general social drift. The
power and virtuosity of the means and machinery of action
can thus hide or obscure the costliness, frivolity or horror of
the end-purposes pursued.

But if, on the one side, "the information society" can
give too little information, on the other side it can give too
much. In his work the individual is fed signals and messages
of a highly preselected and specialized kind. In contrast, in
his leisure and in his personal relations, he receives a vast
mass of assorted signals and messages of a most extraordinary variety.

Cardinal Newman, a century ago, described the mental
life of sailors in terms curiously applicable to the citizen of a
contemporary intensively developed mass-communications
society. "They see visions of great cities and wild regions;
they are in the marts of commerce, or amid the islands of the
South; they gaze on Pompey's pillar or on the Andes; and
nothing which meets them carries them forward or backward, to any idea beyond itself. Nothing has a drift or relation; nothing has a history or a promise. Everything stands
by itself, and comes and goes in its turn, like the shifting

214

scenes of a show, which leaves the spectator where he was."[6]

The information and communications that come to individuals outside their occupational and vocational settings tend to have this character of "meaninglessness," or of utter presentness, of little or no intelligible context, history, or future significance. They are, in Richard Hoggart's phrase, "sensations without commitment." To be sure—and this is a most important qualification to bear in mind if one is not to succumb to the exaggerated and unwarranted cliches about "mass society"—most individuals live in settings in which they are protected against the full impact of this tendency. New information about diets can be checked with one's doctor; advertisements can be discussed with knowing friends; the family looks at the television together; a boy takes some guidance from his peers with respect to drugs or get-rich-quick schemes. The significance of the influential people in the individual's environment in shaping and channeling his reactions to the mass media is one of the facts we *have* learned from empirical sociology. The picture of the individual, naked, helpless and alone, subjected to all the immense pressures of the media, is a bogey, not a reality. Accordingly the impact of mass communications tends to be localized and domesticated.

Nevertheless, the implication of the above remarks is that the problems of leisure, of personal moral values, and of social cohesion and civility, in relation to the mass media, are all fundamentally *environmental* problems. Much depends, that is to say, on the others who are in the individual's immediate surroundings, their knowledge, their character, their permanence on the scene, their relationships to each other and to him. There are, indeed, many people in New York or Tokyo whose aloneness approaches the condition which I described above as a "bogey." It is a "bogey" only as a description of the typical. And there is one particular distortion which is fairly widespread. In contemporary society at large, the maldistribution of one critical resource

—sound professional advice—is one of the greatest sources of social and moral decline.

Indeed, the role of the new, powerful, and centralized media of communication is so crucial in contemporary societies like Japan and the United States, and the specialization of knowledge and technique is also so great, as to undermine two images of man on which much that has been best in Western and Westernized civilization since the seventeenth century has turned. One is "Cartesian man"—rejecting all external authority, examining everything for himself, judging without relying on any brain but his own, taking personal responsibility for every one of his thoughts and beliefs. The other is John Stuart Mill's "Individual," capable of growing in the best direction for himself and society if only he is allowed by society to make his own decisions.

Neither of these images, insofar as they express ideals, can be carelessly discarded. "Cartesian man" expresses a belief in the ultimate sovereignty of the individual mind with regard to the adoption of the individual's fundamental beliefs—an ideal without which the very concept of a liberal civilization as we have come to know it over the last three to four hundred years is almost unintelligible. And Mill's "Individual" speaks to the need for the particularization and localization in morals and politics of general ideas, and for the immeasurably greater desirability of building a society out of strong-minded but tolerant men and women than out of well-disciplined but submissive people, who act according to a central plan. But these ideals must now be supported —and can only be supported—on the basis of a candid recognition of the altered social facts. Cartesian man needs professional advice; his sovereign mind will show itself in the good judgment to choose the right adviser. And Mill's individual, if he is to find and follow his own bent, needs a society that acts affirmatively to provide him with a sustaining environment in which the right advisers for him are available to be chosen.

216

John Stuart Mill assumed a "marketplace of ideas" in which, through competition for the individual's assent, the true and the good would gradually triumph. I do not have any misgivings about the soundness of Mill's warnings against censorship. But the conditions of communication and of the competition of ideas in contemporary society are now so changed that some of Mill's basic presuppositions are questionable. Specifically, the notion that the law and government have a largely negative role with regard to the communications marketplace needs challenge. A general and affirmative public interest in the quality and equity of "the communications environment" seems to me a major requirement. Whether this interest can be made effective while maintaining the First Amendment liberties may well be one of the central and testing issues in the not too distant future.

The most urgent problem, of course, is an educational one. Schooling of a new kind and effectiveness is almost certainly necessary to produce in the citizens of our societies a capacity to navigate in the seas of mass communications, to maintain judgment and discernment, and to understand and respect standards of high performance. But to discuss what is necessary here would lead us into a vast new field. I shall content myself simply with saying that, for a variety of reasons, Japan seems to me to be in a much better position to cope with this problem successfully than the United States. For the moment at least, the moods of the post-World War II period have been reversed. Behind Japanese modesty there is considerable self-confidence; behind the brave words of Americans there is deep malaise. In America, at least, the malaise reflects not simply the exhausting Vietnam experience but a sense that fundamental values hitherto taken for granted are questionable, or, even worse, unmeaning. This malaise is not likely to be cured by rhetorical devices, but only by unsparing philosophical analysis of received ideas. And even that will not be enough. A certain period of rest and rehabilitation, and a noticeable effort at public reconstruction, will also be necessary.

Notes

1. William Wordsworth, *Lyrical Ballads, 1798-1805,* Preface.

2. Webster's New International Dictionary.

3. To be sure, there have been societies, by and large egalitarian in their traditions and austere in their values, e.g., the Jews, the Quakers, which have been exceptions to these generalizations. But these societies have been marked by a powerful indigenous love of learning. There is no evidence that the love of learning (as against the desire for marketable credentials) is among the values spread by mass social democracy.

4. Robin Marris, "Galbraith, Solow, and the Truth about Corporations," *The Public Interest,* no. 11 (Spring 1968): 38.

5. I am not speaking here of the rule of inquiry which distinguishes descriptive statements from normative judgments, and which seems to me indispensable to objective inquiry.

6. J. H. Newman, *The Idea of a University,* Discourse VI. I owe this quotation to Richard Hoggart, who uses it in his *The Uses of Literacy* (London, Chatto and Windus, 1957), p. 159.

Index

221

223

About the Contributors

Charles Frankel, the distinguished educator and author, has consistently combined scholarly work with active involvement in political and public affairs. He is now Old Dominion Professor of Philosphy and Public Affairs at Columbia University.

He received the B.A. in English and Philosophy from Columbia College and did graduate work at Cornell and Columbia Universities. During the war he served in the U.S. Navy in Japan and the Pacific area.

Among the positions which Professor Frankel has held recently are Assistant Secretary of State for Educational and Cultural Affairs and Chairman of the International Committee to Examine French Education, which was established by the French government. From 1958 to 1959, he was host of the CBS educational TV program, "The World of Ideas," and was moderator of CBS Radio's "Invitation to Learning."

Professor Frankel's civic activities include his current membership on the Commission on the Quality, Cost and

Financing of Education of the State of New York. He is currently Chairman of the American Committee of the Intellectual Interchange Program of the Japan Society.

Among his many books are *The Pleasures of Philosophy, High on Foggy Bottom, Education and the Barricades, The Neglected Aspect of Foreign Affairs,* as well as a novel, *A Stubborn Case.* He also contributes to many periodicals and scholarly journals.

Nathan Glazer is an expert on urban planning and urban social problems and has been active in both the academic and publishing fields. He is currently Professor of Education and Social Structure at Harvard University.

Professor Glazer received the M.A. degree in Anthropology and Linguistics at the University of Pennsylvania and the Ph.D. in Sociology from Columbia University. Before starting his teaching career, he was on the staff of *Commentary* magazine and was an editorial advisor for Doubleday Anchor Books as well as for Random House. He was Professor of Sociology at the University of California at Berkeley prior to arriving at Harvard University in 1969.

From 1961 to 1962, Professor Glazer did research on urban planning and social problems in Japan and later made extensive lecture trips to Japan, Korea, and India. He was also consultant to Harvard University's Development Advisory Service in Malaysia in 1970, and was a member of the faculty of the Salzburg Seminar in American Studies in Salzburg, Austria in 1971.

Professor Glazer is the coauthor of *The Lonely Crowd* with David Riesman and Reuel Denny, *Faces in the Crowd* with David Riesman, and *Beyond the Melting Pot* with Daniel Patrick Moynihan, which won the Anisfield-World Award. He is the author of *American Judaism* and, most recently, *Remembering the Answers: Essays on the American Student Revolt.* He is a regular contributor to the *New York Times Sunday Magazine, Commentary,* and *The Public Interest.*

Robert L. Heilbroner, a leading social analyst and economist, is presently Norman Thomas Professor of Economics of the Graduate Faculty of Political and Social Science at the New School for Social Research.

He received the B.A. from Harvard in 1940, and the Ph.D. from the New School.

After World War II, he worked briefly as an economist in private business before beginning his career as an economic essayist, writing for *Harper's* and other magazines. His first book, *The Worldly Philosophers,* has been translated into twenty languages and has sold over a million copies.

Subsequent books include *The Future as History, The Limits of American Capitalism, The Economic Problem,* and *Between Capitalism and Socialism.* In addition, he has lectured on many campuses and before business and labor groups and has appeared extensively on educational television, where he was the moderator for "The Court of Reason."

Heilbroner's two main fields of interest are classical political economy and contemporary trends in capitalism. His most recent contributions include a critical essay on Adam Smith and a new biographical essay on Smith for the *Encyclopaedia Britannica.*

Professor Heilbroner is a member of the editorial boards of *Dissent, Journal of History of Ideas,* and *Social Research.*

Samuel P. Huntington has had an active academic and public career. He is Frank G. Thompson Professor of Government at Harvard and a member of the executive committee of the University's Center of International Affairs. From 1967 to 1971, he was Chairman of the Department of Government.

Professor Huntington, who received the B.A. from Yale University, the M.A. from the University of Chicago, and the Ph.D. from Harvard, began teaching at Harvard in 1951. From 1959 to 1962 he was Associate Director of the Institute of War and Peace Studies at Columbia University. He has served as a consultant to the U.S. Air Force, the U.S. Navy, and the Institute of Defense Analysis. He has chaired both the Study Group on U.S. Security Policy in East Asia at the Brookings Institution and the Council of Vietnamese Studies of the Southeast Asia Development Advisory Group. Currently he is a Fellow of the American Academy of Arts and Sciences, a member of the Council on Foreign Relations and of the Institute of Strategic Studies. He is also coeditor of the quarterly journal, *Foreign Policy.*

His most recent book, *Authoritarian Politics in Modern Society: The Dynamics of Established One-Party Systems,* was edited with Clement H. Moore. His works include *Political Order in Changing Societies, The Soldier and the State: Theory and Politics of Civil-Military Relations* and *The Common Defense: Strategic Programs in National Politics.*

F. Roy Lockheimer, Associate Executive Director of the Japan Society, has been a student of Japanese affairs since he was an undergraduate at Tufts University, where he received the B.A. in History in 1959. He has graduate degrees from the Fletcher School of Law and Diplomacy, with intensive Japanese language preparation at Harvard and Yale. Research took him to Japan in 1962 for a study of conservative party politics at the graduate school of Keio University. For several years as a guest in the household of a conservative party politician, as an Exchange Research Fellow and Lecturer at Keio, and as a columnist for the *Japan Times,* Lockheimer immersed himself in Japanese life and studies. From 1965 to 1966 he was Assistant Professor of History at the University of Wisconsin, where his assignment was to create a regional-campus program in Asian studies. In 1966, he became Associate for Japan of the American Universities Field Staff (AUFS), where he reported from Tokyo on developments in Japan. He joined the Japan Society in 1971 as Associate Executive Director with a major responsibility for program development, public affairs, and educational development. Lockheimer has made several nationwide lecture tours and has published widely in English and Japanese, with a special focus on Japanese politics, foreign relations, economics, science and technology, and population problems.

James William Morley has devoted his life to the study of East Asia, especially Japan and her relations with Asia and the United States throughout his academic career, government service, and other activities. He is Professor of Government at Columbia University and was Director of Columbia's East Asian Institute from 1971 to 1973. He is currently in Japan on leave of absence from Columbia.

After graduating from Harvard in 1943, he studied the Japanese language at the U.S. Naval Language School and Advanced Naval Intelligence School. He received the M.A. in International Relations from Johns Hopkins University and the Ph.D. in East Asian and East European History from Columbia.

While teaching at Columbia, he was a delegate to many conferences on educational and cultural cooperation sponsored by the United States and Japan and spent two years in Tokyo as Special Assistant to the U.S. Ambassador. He is currently a consultant to the State Department.

He is also affiliated with a number of organizations and publications. He is consultant on Japan and Korea for the *Columbia Encyclopaedia*, a member of the Council on Foreign Relations, a Director of the Japan Society and advisory editor to *Journal of International Affairs*.

Morley is the author of *Japan and Korea: America's Allies in the Pacific* and numerous articles and papers. He is the editor of and contributor to *Forecast for Japan: Security in the 1970's; Dilemmas of Growth in Prewar Japan;* and *Japan's Foreign Relations, 1868-1941: A Research Guide.* He is currently serving as editor and partial translator of *Japan's Road to War.*

Ken'ichi Tominaga is a sociologist specializing in change in contemporary industrial society. After receiving the B.A. and M.A. in Sociology from the University of Tokyo, he began his teaching career there. In 1966 he received the Ph.D. from the University of Tokyo and became an Associate Professor.

Professor Tominaga has also participated in numerous international symposiums and projects sponsored by the leading Japanese newspapers. For example, he toured the United States in 1966 for Japan's leading newspaper, *Yomiuri Shinbun*, while making an extensive study of the future of the industrial society.

His major publications in the Japanese language are *The Theory of Social Change and Structure* and *Change of the Industrial Society*. He is also the translator of *Economy and Society*, coauthored by Talcott Parsons and Neil Smelser, and *Class and Class Conflict in an Industrial Society* by Ralf Dahrendorf.

Yoshimi Uchikawa is Director of the Institute of Journalism at the University of Tokyo and is one of the most active Japanese in the fields of journalism and mass communication studies.

Upon graduation from the Department of Politics of the University of Tokyo in 1948, he became a Research Fellow of the Institute of Journalism. He is an active member of the Japan Association of Political Science, the Japan Association of Journalism and Mass Communication Studies, and the International Association of Mass Communication Research, where he is on the Board of Executives.

Professor Uchikawa is the author of *History of Journalism* and the translator into Japanese of *Four Theories of the Press*. In addition, he has contributed many articles on mass communication to periodicals and journals.

Hirofumi Uzawa is a distinguished economist who has traveled widely and taught for many years at American universities. One of the most internationally-minded economists in Japan, Uzawa is currently Professor of Economics at the University of Tokyo.

He studied mathematics at the University of Tokyo and became a Research Associate at the Applied Mathematics and Statistics Laboratories of Stanford University in 1956. Later he taught in the Department of Economics at Stanford Univeristy and the Department of Economics and Mathematics at the University of California, Berkeley. He was Associate Professor of Economics and Statistics at Stanford University and Professor of Economics at the University of Chicago before returning in 1969 to the University of Tokyo.

Professor Uzawa is a fellow of the Econometric Society, Overseas Fellow of Churchill College at Cambridge University, and a fellow of the American Academy of Arts and Sciences.

His English-language publications include *Studies in Linear and Non-Linear Programming,* which he coauthored with K.J. Arrow and L. Hurwicz, and *Readings in the Modern Theory of Economic Growth,* coauthored with J. Stiglitz. Most recently the three-volume work *Price Theory* and *Theory of Economic Development and Fluctuations* have appeared in Japanese. Professor Uzawa has contributed numerous articles to professional journals. He was a Fellow of the Intellectual Interchange Program of the Japan Society in New York in 1972.

Joji Watanuki is a prominent political sociologist specializing in contemporary Japanese political society. Born in Los Angeles, Watanuki was educated in Japan and taught for a number of years in the United States. Currently he is Professor of Sociology at Sophia University. He received the B.A. and M.A. in Sociology from the University of Tokyo.

After teaching at the University of Tokyo, he became a Rockefeller Foundation Fellow and Visiting Fellow at Princeton University from 1962 to 1963. The following year he served as Research Associate at the University of California, Berkeley. He was also Visiting Professor at the

University of Iowa before joining Sophia University's Institute of International Relations in 1971.

Professor Watanuki has published a number of books on contemporary politics, social change, and Japanese political society and has contributed numerous articles to Japanese professional journals. Some of his recent English-language articles include "Social Structure and Political Participation in Japan" in the *Institute of International Relations Research Papers* published by Sophia University in 1972; "State Formation and Nation-building in East Asia" in the *International Social Science Journal* published by UNESCO; and "The Future of Japanese Politics" in the *Annual Review of the Japan Institute of International Affairs*.